Mesopotamia and Iran in the Parthian and Sasanian Periods: Rejection and Revival
c. 238 BC–AD 642

Proceedings of a Seminar in memory of
Vladimir G. Lukonin

Funded by a gift from
Raymond and Beverly Sackler

Edited by John Curtis

Published for The Trustees of
The British Museum by
BRITISH MUSEUM PRESS

In memory of Bernadette Henry
(1958–1999)

© 2000 The Trustees of the British Museum

Published in 2000 by British Museum Press
A division of The British Museum Company Ltd
46 Bloomsbury Street, London WC1B 3QQ

A catalogue record for this book is available from the British Library

ISBN 0 7141 1146 5

Designed and typeset by Martin Richards
Printed and bound in Great Britain by The Bath Press

Front jacket: Silver bowl showing a Sasanian king, probably Bahram V, hunting lions. WA 124092, Franks Bequest.
Back jacket: Pottery jar with stamped designs from Borsippa in Mesopotamia, Sasanian period, 6th century AD. WA 92394.

Contents

Acknowledgments	4
List of Illustrations	5
Preface	7
Introduction *John Curtis*	11
Parthian and Sasanian History of Iran *Richard N. Frye*	17
Parthian Culture and Costume *Vesta Sarkhosh Curtis*	23
The Rock Reliefs of Sasanian Iran *Georgina Herrmann*	35
Sasanian Silver Vessels: The Formation and Study of Early Museum Collections *Prudence O. Harper*	46
Mesopotamia in the Sasanian Period: Settlement Patterns, Arts and Crafts *St John Simpson*	57
Sasanian Art beyond the Persian World *Guitty Azarpay*	67
Bibliography	76
Illustration Acknowledgments	80
Plates	81
Colour Plates	97

Acknowledgements

A number of people have helped with preparing these papers for publication, and grateful thanks are due to all of them. The work on the typescripts was started by Bernadette Heaney, and continued mainly by Brian Blackmun, Rosemary Livermore, and Beverley Fryer. Photographic work in The British Museum was done by Barbara Winter and Lisa Bliss, and the maps were drawn by Ann Searight. Carolyn Jones of British Museum Press has been an exemplary editor and deserves much of the credit for this book. Last but not least it is a great pleasure to record again our thanks to Raymond and Beverly Sackler who not only sponsored this seminar but also encouraged its publication.

List of Illustrations

Figures
1. The speakers at the Fourth Lukonin Memorial Seminar on 14th July 1997. From left: Guitty Azarpay, Georgina Herrmann, Richard Frye, Prudence Harper, St John Simpson and Vesta Sarkhosh Curtis.
2. Boris Marshak, who gave the Lukonin Memorial Lecture in 1996.
3. Raymond and Beverly Sackler (right) with Lord and Lady Egremont at the opening of the Ancient Levant gallery on 16 July 1998.
4. Bernadette Henry (1958–99).
5. The Ancient Near East and surrounding areas.
6. Mesopotamia and Iran showing the more important places mentioned in the text.
7. Seventeenth-century drawing of Parthian rock relief at Bisitun.
8. Bronze statue from Shami.
9. Wall painting at Dura Europos showing figures in Parthian dress.
10. Sketch of the tombs and reliefs at Naqsh-i Rustam.
11. Jousting scene of Hormuzd II at Naqsh-i Rustam.
12. Map showing Sasanian settlement patterns in southern Mesopotamia.
13. The Seleucia-Veh Ardashir-Ctesiphon conurbation.
14. Plan of excavated Sasanian architecture and the nearby fortifications in the southern quarter of Veh Ardashir.
15. The arched facade of the larger rock-cut vault at Taq-i Bustan, near Kermanshah.
16. A winged horse on a late Sasanian silk fragment from Antinoe, Egypt.
17. Detail of design on the interior of a silver-gilt bowl, formerly in the Foroughi collection, showing dancing women in association with vintaging scenes.

Black and white plates
1. Coins of Arsaces II (?) (a); Mithradates I (b-e); Artabanus I (f); Mithradates II (g-i); Phraates IV (j); Artabanus IV (k); Kamnaskires III (l); Orodes II (m); and Gordian III and Abgar (n-o).
2. Ivory rhyton from Old Nisa, in the Historical Museum, Ashkhabad.
3. Lower part of a marble statue from Susa, in the Muzeh Melli, Tehran.
4. Limestone stela from Ashur, in the Archaeological Museum, Istanbul.
5. Stucco decoration from Qaleh-i Yazdigird showing a male figure wearing a pointed hat, tunic and trousers.
6. Stucco column capital from Warka, in the British Museum.
7. Terracotta figurine from Warka, in the British Museum, showing a banqueter dressed in Parthian costume.
8. Gold belt clasp allegedly from the Nahavand area, in the British Museum.
9. Statute of Atalu from Hatra.
10. Relief from Susa showing Artabanus IV, in the Muzeh Melli, Tehran.
11. Rock reliefs at Tang-i Sarvak in Elymais.
12. Coins of Papak and Ardashir I (a), Ardashir I (b) and Ardashir I and his son Shapur (c).
13. Detail from jousting scene at Firuzabad showing Ardashir.

LIST OF ILLUSTRATIONS

14 Horses depicted on a Sasanian relief (III) at Bishapur.
15 Detail from relief of Bahram II at Naqsh-i Rustam showing Kartir.
16 Back wall of large grotto at Taq-i Bustan showing investiture probably of Khusro II.
17 Silver plate, in the Bibliothèque Nationale, Paris, showing a king hunting animals.
18 Silver plate, in the Bibliothèque Nationale, Paris, showing ceremonial scenes.
19 Silver ewer, in the Bibliothèque Nationale, Paris, showing crossed-over lions.
20 Silver vase, in the Museum für Islamische Kunst, Berlin, illustrated with herons and trees.
21 Silver vase, in the British Museum, decorated with vintaging scenes.
22 Silver plate, in the British Museum, showing a banqueting scene.
23 Silver plate, in the British Museum, decorated with a scene of a king hunting lions.
24 Silver vase, in the Muzeh Melli, Tehran, decorated with dancing female figures.
25 Silver bowl, in the Walters Art Gallery, Baltimore, decorated with entertainment scenes and dancing females.
26 Silver bowl, in the Walters Art Gallery, Baltimore, showing a seated king and queen.
27 Silver plate, in the Metropolitan Museum of Art, showing a king hunting rams.
28 Silver plate, in the Freer Gallery of Art, showing a king hunting boars.
29 Drawing of a silver plate, now lost, decorated with a hunting scene.
30 Sasanian stamp seal in the British Museum giving the title 'accountant of Garmekan and Nodh-Ardashirakan' in Middle Persian.
31 An inscribed 'incantation bowl' in the British Museum depicting a symbolically chained Lilith in the centre.
32 The facade of the Taq-i Kisra at Ctesiphon as photographed by Gertrude Bell.
33 Sasanian sword in the British Museum with silver scabbard and crucible steel blade.
34 Stamp impression on a fragmentary Late Sasanian jar excavated at Nineveh, now in the British Museum, showing a stag with a neck-ribbon and a cross.
35 Relief showing the investiture of Ardashir I at Naqsh-i Rustam.
36 Detail from the 'Cup of Solomon', in the Cabinet des Medailles, Bibliothèque Nationale, Paris.
37 Pattern showing a *senmurv* on the robe of Khusro II at Taq-i Bustan.
38 Horn rhyton with gazelle protome, in gilt-silver, in the Arthur M. Sackler Gallery. Height 15.5 cm.
39 Pearl-framed bird motif from a Chinese silk fragment, from the vicinity of Turfan, in Xinjiang, China.
40 Drawing showing the king of Samarkand and a member of his retinue on a seventh-century mural from a Sogdian palace complex at Afrasiab, Samarkand.
41 Sasanian stucco relief, showing a grape-vine with grape cluster, Tepe-i Mil, Iran.

Colour plates

I Head of a painted statue with helmet, in the Historical Museum, Ashkhabad.
II Glazed pottery coffin from Warka, in the British Museum.
III Statue of King Valgash at Hatra.
IV Relief in Bel Temple at Palmyra, showing the god Aglibol.
V Relief at Naqshi-i Rustam showing the investiture of Ardashir.
VI General view of a Sasanian rock relief (III) at Bishapur.
VII Relief at Naqsh-i Rustam showing the victory of Shapur over the Romans.
VIII Sasanian relief at Tang-i Qandil.
IX Silver plate, in the British Museum, decorated with a *senmurv*.
X Silver plate, in the British Museum, showing a king hunting stags.
XI Sasanian seal inscribed in Middle Persian 'reliance on god', illustrating a banqueting scene.
XII Late Sasanian stamped jar.
XIII Sasanian cut-glass tube from Nineveh, early seventh century AD.
XIV Detail of woollen textile from Antinoe, Egypt, restored by Mme Dal Pra.
XV Painted earthenware tomb figurine, showing a Central Asian leading a camel loaded with twists of prepared silk fibres. Height 45cm. From a Tang tomb in the Xsian region.
XVI Earthenware vessel (height 32.5 cm) with three-colour lead glaze, in the shape of a ewer with a phoenix head. Height 32.5 cm. From a Tang tomb in the region of Xsian.
XVII Addorsed roosters' heads on a Sasanian silk fragment from Antinoe, Egypt.
XVIII Detail of an embellished ram on a late Sasanian silk fragment from Antinoe, Egypt.
XIX A winged horse on a late Sasanian silk fragment from Antinoe, Egypt.

Preface

by John Curtis

In this book are gathered together the papers delivered at the fourth seminar held at the British Museum in memory of Vladimir G. Lukonin, the distinguished Russian scholar who was Head of the Oriental Department at the State Hermitage Museum until his untimely death in 1984. The seminar, held on 14 July 1997, was about 'Mesopotamia and Iran in the Parthian and Sasanian Periods', which by a happy coincidence was Vladimir Lukonin's main area of specialisation. Six scholars were brought together (Fig. 1) to talk about various aspects of this subject. After a brief introduction by John Curtis, Professor Richard Frye of Harvard University set the scene by reviewing the history of the Parthian and Sasanian periods, and Vesta Sarkhosh Curtis of the Department of Coins and Medals, British Museum, spoke about Parthian culture and costume. Next, Georgina Herrmann of University College London, and Prudence Harper of the Metropolitan Museum of Art, New York, described the rock reliefs of Sasanian Iran and Sasanian silver vessels respectively. St John Simpson of the Department of Western Asiatic Antiquities, British Museum, then dealt with Sasanian arts and crafts, and the proceedings were brought to a close by Guitty Azarpay of the University of California, Berkeley, who surveyed Sasanian art in

1 The speakers at the Fourth Lukonin Memorial Seminar on 14th July 1997. From left: Guitty Azarpay, Georgina Herrmann, Richard Frye, Prudence Harper, St John Simpson, and Vesta Sarkosh Curtis.

Central Asia. The seminar was followed by a reception and the annual dinner for the Friends of the Ancient Near East, the support group for the Department of Western Asiatic Antiquities.

This seminar was the fourth and last in a series dealing with relations between Mesopotamia and Iran from 3500 BC until the beginning of the Islamic period in the 7th century AD. The papers of the three previous seminars have already been published, and the appearance of this volume completes the publication of all the papers given at the four seminars.

The four seminars were organised in alternate years, with lectures in memory of Vladimir Lukonin being delivered every other year. Thus between the third and fourth seminars, on 15 July 1996, we were privileged to have a lecture from Professor Boris Marshak (Fig. 2) of the State Hermitage Museum in St Petersburg. He has been on the staff of the Oriental Department since 1958, and is now in charge of the Central Asian collection and the Sasanian silver. He is best known for his excavations at the Sogdian site of Penjikent in Tajikistan where spectacular wall paintings have been found. These provided many of the illustrations for his lecture which was on 'Images of the Universe in the Early Medieval Art of Iranian Peoples'. Professor Marshak demonstrated that the art of Sogdia, Tokharistan (Bactria) and Iran in the sixth to eighth centuries AD had a universalist theme, with the artists seeking to convey the idea that people need to be protected by all the elements of the universe. There are traces of this concept in these countries in earlier times, but it is only after AD 500 in Iran and Tokharistan and after AD 650 in Sogdia that we have a large number of works of art with images depicting or symbolising the whole world.

In Sogdia, at Penjikent, Samarkand and Varakhsha, paintings in the palaces and houses of princes, noblemen and merchants show a variety of deities who serve as the divine patrons of the owner. These gods, who are sometimes represented by symbols such as the sun and moon, are shown in close proximity to the world of man which is represented by

2 *Left* Boris Marshak, who gave the Lukonin Memorial Lecture in 1996.

3 *Centre* Raymond and Beverly Sackler (right) with Lord and Lady Egremont at the opening of the Ancient Levant gallery on 16 July 1998.

4 *Right* Bernadette Henry (1958-1999)

epic heroes, noble banqueters and hunters. These paintings, then, symbolise the participation of the whole world in the rites and celebrations of the owner's family.

The relief decoration on stone slabs from three funerary beds from North China dating from the second half of the sixth century AD shows Sogdian colonists amongst representatives of various countries who participate in the burial or memorial services, thus again demonstrating universalism.

In Sasanian Iran the imagery on silver vessels includes various composite beings with different elements of animals and birds symbolising the unity of all kinds of creation. There are also compositions with waters, mountains, trees and plants. Particularly popular in Sasanian art were allegorical symbols of day and night and the four seasons. The reliefs in the large grotto at Taq-i Bustan demonstrate the universal power of the Sasanian king who was equally successful on land and in water, and in both war and peace.

Then, in the year after the fourth Seminar, on 14 July 1998, we were pleased to be able to welcome Dr Mikhail Piotrovsky, Director of the State Hermitage Museum in St Petersburg since 1992, to give the sixth Lukonin Memorial Lecture. This was particularly appropriate as his father, Academician Boris Piotrovsky, Director of the Stage Hermitage 1964–1990, had delivered the first Lukonin Memorial Lecture in 1989 on 'Ancient Iran and the Caucasus'. Dr Piotrovsky spoke about 'Iranian Civilisations and Collections in the State Hermitage, St Petersburg', a subject which was of topical interest owing to the recent publication of Geraldine Norman's book on *The Hermitage: the Biography of a Great Museum* (London 1997). He described the Iranian collections in the State Hermitage starting with objects of Achaemenid and Graeco-Bactrian origin in the so-called Siberian collection of Peter the Great. He went on to talk about some of the highlights of the collection, including the unparalleled Sasanian silver vessels, the ivory rhytons from Nisa near Ashkhabad in Turkmenistan, the frescoes from Penjikent in Tajikistan, the Pazyryk carpet, and the Islamic art and illuminated manuscripts. He described how after the Revolution specialists in oriental studies enjoyed more ideological freedom than scholars in other branches of the humanities, with the result that a number of outstanding people in the Hermitage were attracted to this field. They included Yakov Smirnov, Iusif Orbeli who became Director of the Museum 1934–51, Camilla Trever, Leon Gyuzalyan, Vladimir Lukonin and Evgeny Zeymal, as well as a number of scholars who are all still alive. The lecture was enlivened by some remarkable anecdotes. One story, possibly apocryphal, was about Orbeli's determination to protect his colleagues. He was summoned by the regional committee of the communist party to answer charges that there were too many people from aristocratic families on the staff of the Hermitage. Orbeli responded that he himself was descended from Caucasian nobility that traced its ancestry back for seven or eight centuries, so he could hardly be expected to know anything much about Russian noble families which only went back 400 or 500 years. The officials were taken aback, and did not press their case. Orbeli's loyalty to his staff paid dividends, as became clear when we were told that on a different occasion Gyuzalyan refused to sign a document incriminating Orbeli.

As is well known to participants in these seminars and to readers of these volumes, the Lukonin seminars and lectures have been made possible through a generous gift from Raymond and Beverly Sackler. They have also contributed to the cost of producing these volumes, and they have also sponsored a series of new galleries at the British Museum, the latest of which, devoted to the Ancient Levant, opened on 16 July 1998 (Fig. 3). In this way they have given a great boost to ancient Near Eastern studies. But their interest and support have not stopped there. As explained in the last volume, in 1997 they set up the Raymond and Beverly Sackler Scholar Programme in Ancient Iranian Studies. This allows the British Museum to award an annual scholarship to a young scholar to enable them to work for six months in the Department of Western Asiatic Antiquities. The holders of the first two scholarships have been Katrien Rutten of the University of Gent and Gabriele Puschnigg of University College London respectively.

Both the British Museum and students of Iranian Archaeology have good reason to be deeply grateful to the Sacklers and their generosity and imagination have also set an example for others. Thus, it is a pleasure to record here that the London-based Iran Heritage Foundation has also sponsored a series of awards. These are annual IHF Fellowships at the British Museum, and allow an Iranian scholar to study in the British Museum for a period of three months. The holder of the first Fellowship, in 1998, was Zahra Jaffar-Mohammadi of the Muzeh Melli, Tehran.

It is gratifying to be able to report these positive developments, but at the same time Iranian Archaeology has suffered some losses. Firstly, Ali Hakemi, the excavator of Shahdad, died in Rome on 7 July 1997. He spent his last years in London, and was a regular attender at the Lukonin Lectures and Seminars. Secondly, Dr. Evgeny Zeymal, who was in charge of the Ancient Near Eastern and East Hellenistic collections in the Oriental Department of the State Hermitage Museum in St. Petersburg, died on 6 May 1998. He will be remembered for his work on Central Asian coinage and the Oxus Treasure. He was a colleague and close friend of Vladimir Lukonin, who was Head of the Oriental Department 1964–84, and although he was never able to attend any Lukonin lectures or seminars, he was an ardent supporter of the initiatives which led to the establishment of the Ancient Persia Fund and the Lukonin lectures and seminars.

Lastly, it is sad to have to record that, during the latter stages of the preparation of this book, Bernadette Henry (Fig. 4) passed away. She died from cancer on 10 March 1999 at the tragically early age of 41. She played a large part in organising the Lukonin seminars and lectures and in preparing subsequent volumes for the press. Bernadette was born near Swinford, County Mayo, Republic of Ireland, on 17 February 1958. She began her career at the British Museum in 1978, and moved to the Department of Western Asiatic Antiquities in 1979. There, she served as Personal Secretary to three successive Keepers of the Department, Edmond Sollberger, Terence Mitchell and myself. She will be sadly missed and this volume is dedicated to her memory.

Introduction

by John Curtis

Previous seminars in this series have dealt with relations between Mesopotamia and Iran in the period 3500–1600 BC, then 1600–539 BC, and most recently, in 1995, in the Achaemenid Persian period. The present seminar carries the story down through Parthian and Sasanian times to the Islamic conquest in the seventh century AD. This means, however, that the Hellenistic period, which lasted for 200 years from about 331 BC to 141 BC, has not been covered, so to try and make up for this omission we will concentrate on it in this brief introduction.[1]

The story of Alexander's conquest of the east is well-known. In 334 BC he crossed the Hellespont with a Macedonian army, and he defeated armies of the last Achaemenid Persian king, Darius III, first at the River Granicus, then at Issus, and finally at Gaugamela in Northern Iraq in 331 BC. This last defeat is vividly shown on a mosaic at Pompeii. Gaugamela has been identified with a modern village called Gogomel or Tell Gomel (Reade 1998: 65–6), which is in fact just over 60 kilometres from Erbil and not close to the city as is often stated. Darius himself fled to eastern Iran and was eventually stabbed to death near Damghan by men who had once supported him.

After Gaugamela, the way was now open for Alexander to march into southern Mesopotamia and then Iran. First he looted Susa, and then burnt Persepolis. Now the whole of Mesopotamia and much of the Iranian plateau was under his control. After Alexander's death in 323 BC, however, his generals quarrelled over the division of his empire. In the east Seleucus emerged victorious, and Mesopotamia and Iran became part of the Seleucid Empire and were administered from Seleucia on the Tigris in Mesopotamia. Mints for the production of coins were established at Seleucia itself, Nisibis, Babylon, Susa, Ecbatana (Hamadan), Antioch (Spasinu Charax), Hecatompylus (Shahr-i Qumis), and further east at Bactra (Mørkholm 1991: 117, map 4). In political terms there was strong central control but at the same time a number of local dynasts were allowed to flourish.

There has been much debate about the impact of Hellenism on the Near East, and the

INTRODUCTION

matter is still far from resolved. What can be said, however, is that at a number of sites in southern Mesopotamia, both previously existing centres and new foundations, there is evidence for strong Hellenistic influence. This is shown by the use of the Greek language, Greek currency, Greek influence in the minor arts and crafts, and buildings in Greek style such as gymnasiums and theatres. Amongst the centres where this sort of influence can be found are Dura Europos, Seleucia on the Tigris, Babylon, Borsippa, Warka and Nippur. At Seleucia on the Tigris the street layout based on the characteristic Greek or Hippodamean grid plan is clearly visible (Quarantelli 1985: fig. on p. 89). Also, many of the small finds from Seleucia, such as a stone figurine showing a naked woman reclining and a limestone statuette of a woman dressed in a himation (Quarantelli 1985: nos 233–4, figs on pp. 341, 343) show evidence of Hellenistic influence, although some of the pieces actually date from the Parthian period. The same applies to a statue of the Greek god

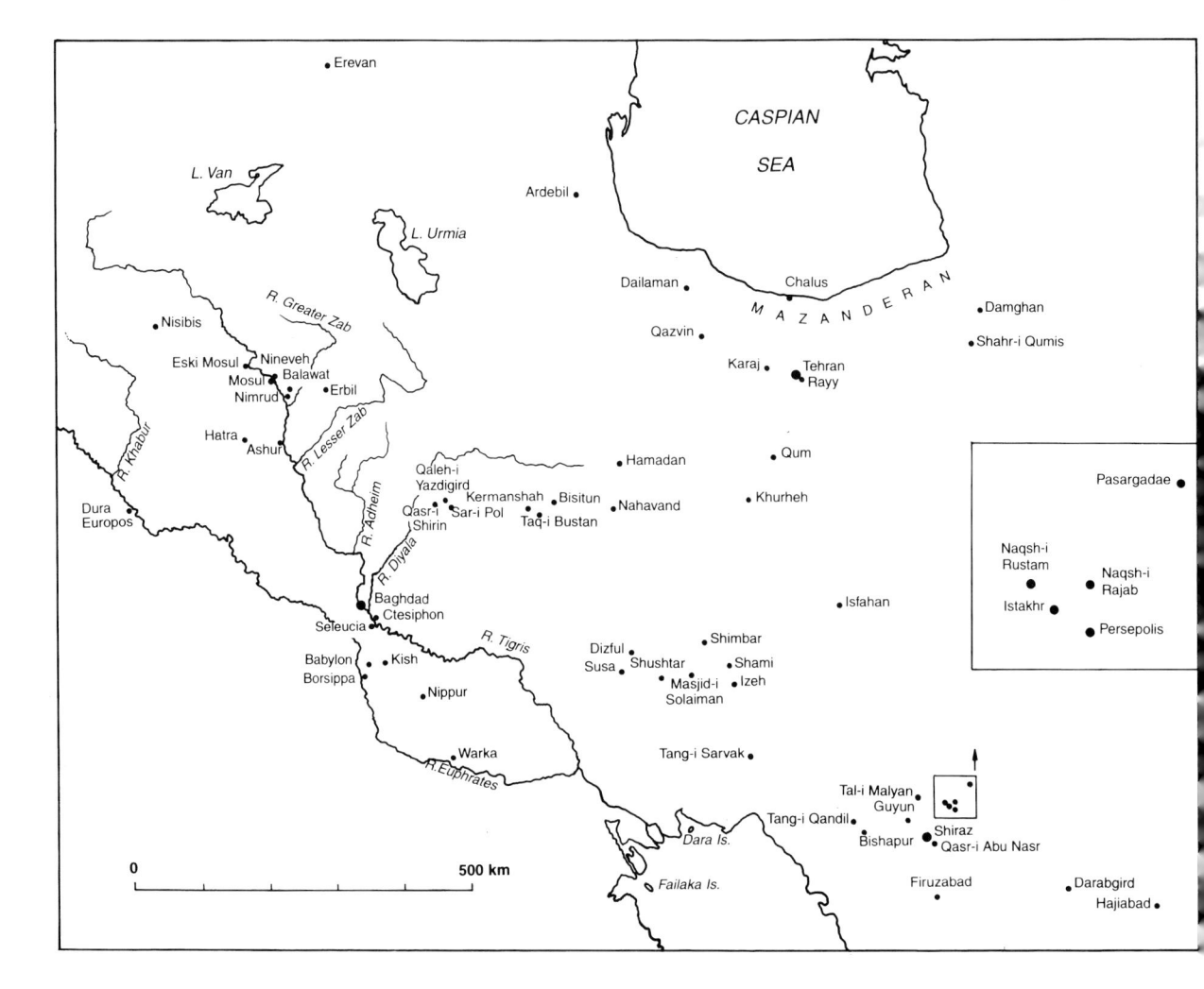

5 The Ancient Near East and surrounding areas.

INTRODUCTION

Heracles that was found at Seleucia. It has a lengthy Greek inscription of AD 150–51 recording that the statue was brought from Mesene by Vologases III or IV following a victory over the local king Mithradates and set up in the Temple of Apollo (Quarantelli 1985: no. 231, figs on pp. 340–41). At Babylon there is a well-preserved theatre with both the plan and the gypsum decoration executed in the Greek style (Koldewey 1914: figs 253–4). From Babylon there are also large numbers of statuettes in clay and stone which clearly reflect Hellenistic influence. For example, there is in the British Museum collection a stone

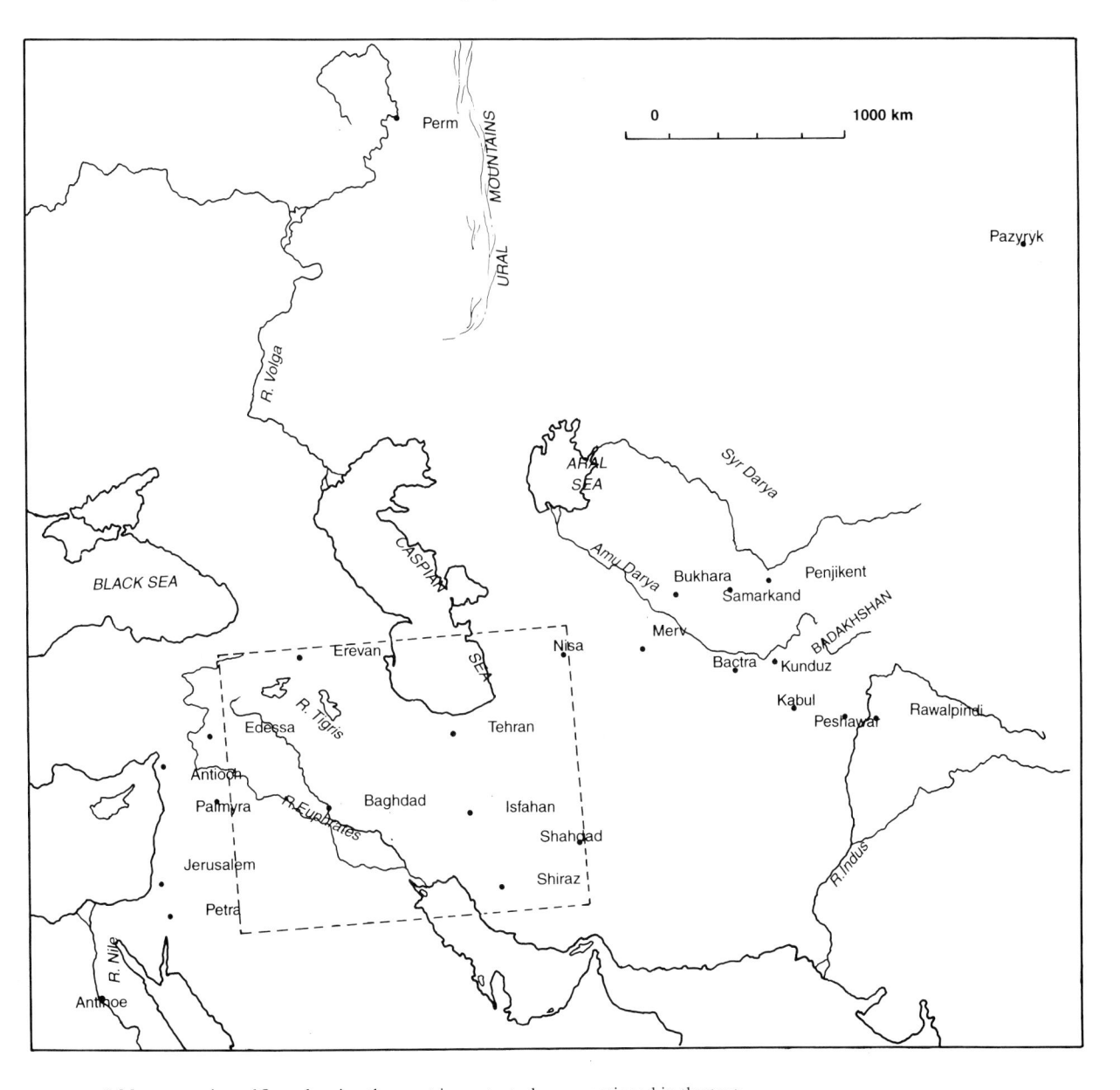

6 Mesopotamia and Iran showing the most important places mentioned in the text.

figure of a woman dressed in a himation (BM 91593), and moulded clay figures also in the British Museum show Europa riding on a bull, a woman in a himation and a chiton, and a pair of children playing musical instruments (BM 91782, 121207, 91794; Karvonen-Kannas 1995: nos 85, 274, 326, pls 55, D, F). Also probably from Babylon are alabastrons which seem to have contained spices. This is indicated by Greek inscriptions on them.

The Seleucid period in Babylonia was a flourishing time for science and literature, as testified by the large number of clay tablets, mostly from Babylon, that have survived. As well as texts dealing with mathematics, astronomy and medicine, there are others that list historical events and there are even students' exercise tablets. One of these (BM 34816) has on one side incantations against evil spirits written in Sumerian and Babylonian and on the other side the text is written phonetically in Greek letters. Amongst the more significant tablets in the British Museum collection, there is one dating from 164 BC that contains observations of Halley's Comet (BM 41462), while another gives a list of Hellenistic and Seleucid kings from Alexander to Antiochus II (BM 35603).

The situation in northern Iraq is much less clear. Again there is evidence for Hellenistic occupation at most of the major sites, but the grand buildings that have been found in Babylonia are on the whole lacking. At Nimrud, for example, there is a succession of Hellenistic villages in the area of the Nabu temple. These were excavated by David and Joan Oates in the years 1955 to 1957 (Oates, D. and J., 1958). A large quantity of Hellenistic pottery was discovered, including stamped amphora handles with Greek inscriptions and large storage jars, some Hellenistic figurines and Hellenistic coins. Hellenistic pottery has also been found in some quantities at other former Assyrian sites like Balawat. At Nineveh there are certainly traces of the Hellenistic period but, probably owing to the chequered history of excavation at the site, the overall picture is not clear (Reade 1998).

The situation in the countryside is also obscure, but some light has been thrown on it by recent excavations particularly in the Eski Mosul area. In 1985 a British Museum expedition working in the Eski Mosul Dam Salvage Project excavated two small Hellenistic sites known as Tell Deir Situn and Grai Darki (Curtis, Green and Knight 1987–8). At Tell Deir Situn, located on a low outcrop and surrounded on three sides by a wadi, stone wall footings of a rectangular building nearly 18 metres long were uncovered. The walls were about 1 metre thick, which would be completely out of place in an ordinary small village. Therefore, it seems that this building might have been a small fort or perhaps a police post. In the building at Tell Deir Situn a good deal of pottery was found. It includes forms painted in red or black and bowls and fish plates of the kind distinctive of the Hellenistic period. Some of the sherds were stamped with different kinds of floral motif. The Hellenistic date of the site was confirmed by the fortunate discovery of a coin associated with the latest phase of the building. It is of the king Alexander Balas (150–145 BC) and was minted at Antioch. On the reverse it shows a naked Apollo holding a bow and arrow. Other finds from Tell Deir Situn include a collection of terracotta loomweights, mostly with oval stamps on the top, a 'fish-tail' pottery lamp, and a terracotta figurine showing a male figure wearing a belted tunic and with a cloak over his shoulder. At the nearby site of Grai Darki there was again a rich collection of typically Hellenistic pottery which includes some interesting forms as well as painted sherds. Also at Grai Darki were found two large circular pits that were presumably originally grain silos.

It is interesting that there are a number of other sites in this area with Hellenistic occupation, whereas sites from the preceding and following periods seem to be much less common. One possible explanation is that in antiquity, as today, the area was fairly wild and unruly and it was only in the Hellenistic period that there was a sufficient degree of security to encourage permanent settlement. This would explain the fort at Tell Deir Situn. Also, the presence at Grai Darki of grain silos – and at other sites in the area – seems to indicate that the rich agricultural resources of the area were being exploited at this time.

Traces of the Seleucid period in Iran are rather more elusive than they are in Mesopotamia, but nevertheless there is a growing body of evidence. We know in any case of the foundation or refoundation of Hellenistic cities, notably at Susa, Hamadan, Rayy and Shahr-i Qumis. Further south, commercial reasons led to the foundation of cities around the head of the Persian Gulf such as on the island of Ikaros (now Failaka) and at Spasinu Charax. At Hamadan the recent excavations of Dr M.S. Sarraf have uncovered a large building which could well be Hellenistic in origin (Sarraf 1997: fig. 4)[2] but pottery and small finds are scarce. They are more numerous at Susa which became a Greek city or *polis* with a Greek municipal structure, a gymnasium, and so on. Evidence for Greek presence here was found even during the earliest excavations at the site, those of the British archaeologist W.K. Loftus in 1850–52. For example, in the southern part of the 'Ville Royale', known as the 'Donjon', Loftus found a small column base with a square pedestal on which was a Greek inscription (Curtis, J.E., 1993: 11, pl. 76). This is a memorial to the Greek governor of Susa from his friend Pythagoras, son of Aristarchus. Because the inscription was upside down Loftus thought it had been carved in this way, but more probably the parts of the column base were not in their original positions when they were found. Loftus also discovered two fragments of a small alabaster statuette of a woman in Greek dress. She wears a chiton with V-shaped neckline under a himation (Curtis, J.E., 1993: 26, no. 77, pls 11a, 18e).[3]

A number of temples were built in the Hellenistic period, reflecting the introduction of new cults. Thus a stone inscription of Antiochus III of 193 BC records the establishment of a cult at Nahavand for his wife Laodicea. From the shrine at Shami, which continued into Parthian times, the excavations of Sir Aurel Stein produced fragments of a bronze head that has been identified as a Seleucid king (Stein 1940: 150–1, pl. IV), possibly Antiochus IV (175–164 BC).[4] It used to be thought that two standing columns with Ionic capitals at Khurheh to the south-west of Qum were part of a Hellenistic temple (Herzfeld 1941: 283–6, pls LXXXVIII – LXXXIX), but it is now believed they belong to a small palace of the Parthian period (Rahbar 1999).

Amongst other monuments of the Hellenistic period, there is the famous stone lion at Hamadan, unfortunately now very eroded. It is much visited by the inhabitants of

Hamadan, including newly-married couples. It has been convincingly argued by the German scholar Heinz Luschey that this lion was set up on the orders of Alexander himself to commemorate his general Hephaestion who died in Hamadan. He compares it to the lions on memorial monuments at Chaeronea and Amphipolis in Greece dating from the second half of the fourth century BC (Luschey 1968). Then, we have the statue of a reclining Heracles at Bisitun (Colledge 1977: fig. 39). This is dated by an inscription to 148 BC, just prior to the capture of Hamadan by the Parthians under Mithradates I. Incidentally, the head of this statue was stolen a few years ago, but happily it has now been recovered.

These are spectacular monuments, but more often Hellenistic presence and influence are recorded through the more humble medium of pottery and potsherds. This is the case at the once important Achaemenid capital city of Pasargadae where a large amount of Hellenistic pottery was found on the Tall-i Takht (Stronach 1978: 183–5, figs 106–22). At Persepolis, on the plain below the terrace, are the remains of buildings including a temple which are ascribed to the Frataraka who were local dynasts in the Hellenistic and Parthian periods (Colledge 1977: fig. 16c).

From the middle of the third century BC onwards the Eastern Seleucid empire came under increasing pressure from the Iranian dynasty of the Parthians, and by 141 BC the Parthians were more or less in complete control of Iran and Mesopotamia. Herzfeld (1941: 275) has observed that 'there is no deeper caesura in the 5000 years of history of the ancient East than the conquest of Alexander the Great, and there is no archaeological object produced after that period that does not bear its stamp'.[5] The case here is surely overstated, but there is no doubt that much Hellenistic influence is discernible in the succeeding Parthian and Sasanian periods. It gradually diminished, however, and it is arguable whether Hellenism made any lasting impression on the Orient. But memories of Alexander himself lingered on. He is often represented in miniature paintings, and in later Persian literature he is sometimes regarded as the half-brother of Darius III (Curtis, V.S., 1993b: 56–9).

Notes

1 For general surveys of the Hellenistic period, see Kuhrt and Sherwin-White 1987, Sherwin-White and Kuhrt 1993, and the *Cambridge History of Iran* 3 (I) (Cambridge 1983).

2 See also Curtis, V.S., and Simpson 1997: 139–40, and Boucharlat 1998.

3 For a brief survey of subsequent French excavations in the Hellenistic levels at Susa, see Amiet 1988: 139–45.

4 For references, see Sherwin-White 1984.

5 Thanks are due to Michael Roaf for reading this section and reminding me of this quotation.

Parthian and Sasanian History of Iran

by Richard N. Frye
HARVARD UNIVERSITY

The first question one should ask is: how did these two dynasties receive their names? The Parthians, in the manner of the times, probably adopted the name of their ruling family, the Arsacids, who were so called after their first king, Arsaces or Arshak. Arsaces may have proclaimed himself sovereign of the province of the Achaemenid and Seleucid empires which was called Parthia (*Parthava* in Old Persian), contemporary Khurasan. The date of this event is disputed, but the year 247 BC, when the Parthian era of time reckoning began, is a good guess. Classical accounts tell us that the first ruler was formerly the leader of a nomadic band called the Parni, who invaded Parthia from the north and settled down, adopting the name and language of the settled people. So there is no mystery about the names Parthians, as they are called in Classical sources, or Arsacids, as eastern sources name them.

The Seleucid kings, successors of Alexander the Macedonian, ruled Iran at that time, but because of their concern with the western part of the Near East, with the twin capitals of Antioch (in Syria) and Seleucia (in Iraq), and constant wars with the Ptolemies of Egypt and other monarchs of the area, Seleucid power had waned in the east. At much the same time as the rise of the Parthians, the Graeco-Macedonian settlers of Bactria, present-day Afghanistan and Tajikistan, threw off allegiance to the Seleucids and the Graeco-Bactrian kingdom came into existence.

It is fascinating that throughout history, most conquerors on the Iranian plateau not only followed much the same trade routes to the east, but they adopted similar policies of building military settlements or cantonments, apart from the towns of the natives. The British were following an ancient tradition when they did the same in the sub-continent of

India, with Delhi and New Delhi, Lahore and Lahore Cantonment, Peshawar and Peshawar Cantonment. Both the Seleucids and later the Arabs did the same, but not, it seems, the Parthians and Sasanians.

Many scholars have characterised the Parthian state as an Oriental reaction against their Graeco-Macedonian predecessors, but the early Arsacids were philhellenes, and their Iranian 'nationalism' was more an attempt to absorb Hellenic settlers, as well as Hellenic culture, into the sea of Iranian inhabitants.

Nevertheless the Parthian aristocracy, although true to their nomadic background (witness the 'Parthian shot' feared by the Romans) can hardly be described as the early models of the later Turkomans, for the capitals of the Parthians moved west as they advanced, and became the heirs of the Seleucids. In so doing they encountered the Romans, who expanded eastward from Syria into Mesopotamia. The latter became the usual battle ground between the two great powers. The centralised empire of the Romans contrasted sharply with the loose, 'feudal' organisation of the Parthians, and at the end of Parthian rule the advantage was strongly on the Roman side.

It is important to remember, however, that in spite of the struggle between the two powers, small states in the 'Fertile Crescent' favoured the Parthian form of government, and they developed greatly as mercantile centres of international trade. The first two centuries of our era was an age of commerce, and the oasis states of the 'Fertile Crescent' flourished as never previously. This was the time of the 'caravan cities' of Petra, Palmyra, Hatra, and the commercially oriented kingdoms of Adiabene or Hadyabh, Characene, Elymais, Gerrha on the western shore of the Gulf, and other trading emporia. Yet strangely our sources from this time are conspicuous by their absence. Indeed the second century is a dark period in our history of the entire region, from the rivers of Mesopotamia to the plains of the sub-continent of India. This is a great pity, for when the curtain rises again from the darkness in the early third century we find a different world. Let me explain.

Inscriptions, and contemporary writings from the east in the pre-second century era, are enigmatic. The few Parthian language remains we have remind us that the heritage of writing in the Achaemenid Empire, which ruled the east, was still very much alive. In fact, there is considerable debate as to whether the literary remains, scant though they are, should be read as broken-down Aramaic, or as Parthian, written in a form of Aramaic script. For the writings are quite close to the imperial Aramaic which was the official written *lingua franca* of the Achaemenid Empire. Notice that I said 'written', for it is difficult to believe that on the Iranian plateau the common spoken tongue was Aramaic. The official spoken language must have been Parthian, even though many dialects and other languages existed. Not until the Sasanian period do we find Parthian written in a form which cannot be mistaken for Aramaic. Probably a reform of writing came in the enigmatic second century, although, of course, we have no evidence. Changes are seen with the advent of the Sasanians, but it is probable that the changes were progressing before the establishment of the new dynasty in 224 of our era. Whence came the name for the new dynasty?

Archaeologists have excavated an early Parthian capital, Nisa, just east of present

Ashkhabad, and ostraca have revealed many interesting items about the early Parthians. Among the names on some of the ostraca we find that of Sasan, which everyone has assumed was the same name as the ancestor of the next Iranian dynasty, and the compound names 'given by Sasan' and others, suggest a theophoric name. But the Parthian language does not distinguish between long and short vowels, so the name could be read as Sisin or Sesen, and Martin Schwartz of the University of California has plausibly suggested that we should in fact consider the name at Nisa to be a minor Semitic deity, known from ancient Ras Shamra to much later Jewish and Christian times, rather than claiming that the one who gave his name to the new dynasty is to be identified with a Parthian deity called Sasan.[1] The latter name does appear on coins of a Parthian ruler in the northwest of India, in the first century of our era, but not as a theophoric one.

According to the tri-lingual royal inscription of Shapur, carved on the Ka'bah of Zoroaster at Naqsh-i Rustam in Fars province, his grandfather Papak was a local king, while his father Ardashir was King of Kings of Iran, and Shapur himself was King of Kings of Iran and non-Iran, or lands outside of the Iranian plateau. What about Sasan? Several sources suggest that Sasan came to Persia or Fars province from the east. That he was a descendant of the Achaemenid rulers is possible, but it may have been the usual propaganda, which repeats itself so many times in the history of Iran, namely that the founder of a new dynasty had royal blood of a previous dynasty. It should be noted that although Sasan is mentioned in the inscriptions as a 'lord' rather than a king, he is not designated as the father of Papak, or great-grandfather of Shapur. The much later historian Tabari, writing in Arabic, assumes that Sasan was the father of Papak, while Middle Persian writings, and Greek sources, tell us that Sasan was in fact a vagabond who, coming to Fars from the east, and because of his charisma and descent from the Achaemenids, was able to insinuate himself into the local ruling family and have an affair with the wife of Papak. Or in another version he created a fictitious connection by marriage with a royal house in Fars. But then we have the story of the accession to the Achaemenid throne of Darius, as found on the Bisitun inscription, and in Herodotus, a story which has been declared fictitious by some scholars. So whom or what do we believe? As I have said on many occasions, perhaps we here are far removed from Leopold von Ranke's assertion that history is the recording of what actually happened, or even from the French positivists who claimed that history was only what people thought had happened. In Iran history may be more what people thought should have happened.

Let me suggest a possible scenario which would save Tabari's reputation. Suppose that Papak was an ambitious and energetic person with pretension to power but without royal blood in his veins. Sasan, a reputed prince, who had come to Fars from the east, did claim to have a respected genealogy, which apparently was accepted, and either he or Papak obtained a religious position as head of a shrine dedicated to Anahita near Istakhr. Inasmuch as Sasan had no son, his daughter was given in marriage to Papak and from this union Ardashir was born. Thus Sasan was the grandfather of Ardashir but not the father of Papak. We may further suggest that another son, Shapur, was afterwards born to Papak from another wife, and that it was this son who succeeded Papak. Ardashir, his half-brother, did not accept this succession, but Shapur's accidental death removed any obstacle for Ardashir who became ruler and adopted the dynastic name from Sasan, after his maternal grandfather. And since descent was reckoned in the male line there was no need for Shapur to explain in his inscription that Sasan was his maternal grandfather.[2] This reconstruction is hypothetical, but it is an attempt to unite the inscription with other written sources. There remains some doubt about Ardashir's descent, yet there is one possible support for this reconstruction.

When Narseh, son of Shapur I, claimed the throne against Bahram III, his Paikuli inscription seems to refer to the time of the conflict between Ardashir and Shapur as a prior justification for his accession (Humbach and Skjaervø 1978–83). If after the death of Hormizd I, eldest son of Shapur, King of Kings, Narseh had been the next oldest son, but Bahram I, a younger son by the same or another mother, and afterwards his son Bahram II succeeded to the throne, then Narseh must have felt cheated and seized the opportunity of the death of Bahram II to assert his claim, which was successful. This might explain why in an inscription at Bishapur, Narseh had Bahram's name erased and his own substituted, and also why there were revolts during Bahram II's reign, possibly connected with claims of legitimacy. Admittedly this is unconfirmed, but at least it does tie up some unexplained facts into a reasonable narrative.

In any case, in the third century the world was changing. Religious orthodoxy was being established by the Christian church, the Jewish Talmudic establishment, and the rise of a Zoroastrian 'state church', if we may very loosely use a modern term. Perhaps all of these developments were spurred by the new upstart religion of Manichaeism, which proclaimed a fixed written orthodoxy of its founder. In both Sasanian Iran and the late Roman Empire the sacralisation of traditions proceeded apace, an important feature of settled monarchies, as opposed to the *laissez-faire* of nomadic traditions. Centralisation replaced local rule, and the caravan cities saw their demise. One by one they fell to the rising power of the Sasanians, and the Romans were not long in following suit in their absorption of Petra and then Palmyra. At least the old pattern of war between east and west continued, and the Sasanians proved more worthy opponents of the Romans than the Parthians.

The wars between the Romans and Persians did not end with the establishment of Byzantium as the new capital of the empire in the east, and not until the Arabs ended the Sasanian Empire, and took away the Byzantine possessions in the east and north Africa, in the seventh century, did another new face of the Near East emerge.

The Sasanians seem to have codified a near-caste system in their society. The nobles and the religious establishment dominated, while artisans and peasants were the under class. It is noteworthy that merchants held a low place in Sasanian society, much the same as artisans, and only at the end of the dynasty did merchants begin to assume an important role in the Sasanian state. In this they were in a sense following their eastern neighbours of the oasis states of Central Asia, where in Bactria, Sogdiana, Khoresmia, and eastern Turkistan, merchants took the place of the landed nobility in importance. In one respect, however, the Sasanian government was aware of economic forces, for their silver coinage maintained a high standard of purity throughout the period of Sasanian rule, with only a few brief periods of debasement. Other states, including the Roman Empire, frequently resorted to debasement of coins which, of course, did not redound to their credit in international trade. The Chinese of the Tang dynasty were well aware of this, since it is interesting that Sasanian silver coins have been found in China, but not the debased coins of the Sogdians, Hephtalites, or other petty states.

What was the heritage of the Parthians and the Sasanians? Even though the two were enemies, yet they should be considered together as the harbingers of the rebirth of Iran after the hiatus of Graeco-Macedonian rule, which brought a new culture and civilisation to the east, similar to the impact of the West in recent times. The difference between the Parthians and Sasanians in a nutshell can be characterised as the preponderance of a Central Asian nomadic mentality, in the case of the Parthians, as contrasted with the Persian settled, imperial mentality, an inheritance from the Achaemenids. Generally this signifies that the Parthians were attuned to the nomadic tradition of conquest by confederation, with all able-bodied men of the tribe as their army, and a relaxed attidude to religion, as well as heroic tales instead of history to describe their past. The Sasanians, on the other hand, believed in conquest by the extension of their own territory, and the appointment of family members as governors in a centralised state. They favoured a more professional army, and were not tolerant in religious matters. Unfortunately, records of the Achaemenids were gone, and memories became mixed with the heroic tales of the Parthians. The Sasanians tried to reconstruct their history by identifying some of the figures in the east-Iranian heroic tradition with names in the Avesta, sacred book of the Zoroastrians, which was not well understood by Sasanian times. The result is an epic history of the Iranian past, recorded in detail by the poet Firdowsi in his book the *Shahnameh*. But at least the Persians had an ancient history, however fanciful, which was more than their neighbours in Mesopotamia and the Egyptians, both of whom had their pasts erased, first by Christianity and then by Islam. For the universal religions believed that real history began with their advent, and that what went before was an age of ignorance, or unimportant in the destiny of mankind. So the legacy of the Parthians and the Sasanians was more than the history of the Iranian plateau, since that continuous record, from the beginning of the world, went into Islamic history, and even to North Africa into the history of the Maghribi historian and sociologist Ibn Khaldun.

Why did the Sasanian Empire fall to the Arabs from the desert? There are many reasons, such as the exhaustion of army and people from the destructive wars with Byzantium, the attraction of a new and dynamic religion, and so on. One important reason was the attraction of a new classless, egalitarian society preached by the Arabs, but hardly practised. For the caste system of the Sasanians was bankrupt and the time was ripe for change. It should be noticed that the Arabs encountered much more resistance in Central Asia than in Persia, but later the inhabitants of the oases of Bukhara, Samarkand and elsewhere adopted Islam with much greater alacrity than the people of the Sasanian Empire, who continued with the ghetto-like divisions of society which obtained in the past. That division of society had come into being when religion became the dominant factor in identification of individuals, rather than allegiance to a ruler or any kind of nationalism. But that is another story. We are only concerned with the overall history of the Parthians and Sasanians, and others will tell of their artistic and other legacies to the world.

Appendix

Sasanian wisdom according to the *'ahd Ardashir*:[3]

> Know that the secret chief of the religion, and the official ruler of the kingdom cannot ever co-exist in a country, without the chief of religion disputing with the head of the country the power he possesses. Because religion is the base, and kingship the pillar (of state), and the lord of the base has more right to the entire structure than he who is lord of the pillar.

Also Ardashir's advice to his son Shapur I:

> Know my son that state and church are twins, and one cannot exist without the other. For religion is the basis of the state, and the king is the guardian of the religion. Be responsive to the needs of religious people. If you neglect and oppress them, among the people of religion will appear secret leaders, from among those whom you have tyrannised, deprived of their rights and humiliated.

Notes

1 Schwartz first proposed this at the meeting of the Society of European Iranists at Cambridge, England, in September 1996. He hopes to publish his findings in the *Bulletin of the Asia Institute* dedicated to V.A. Livshits.

2 If one wished to be more audacious and make guesses about the identity of some of the women mentioned in Shapur's inscription, then one could suggest the following: According to the inscription we have four names of the generation of Papak and his parents – Sasan, Denak mother of Papak, and Rodak, mother of Ardashir, as well as Papak. How do they fit together? Sasan could have married Denak, mother of Papak, and perhaps Rodak, mother of Ardashir, was a sister of Papak. This would be the simplest way of explaining the names in the inscription. Or Rodak may have been a second wife of Papak, as I suggested. Other possibilities are instances of incest, and silence about them in the inscription. Ardashir was the son of Rodak who, as mentioned, may have been sister of Papak, or perhaps married to him or a concubine. Papak probably had another wife, not mentioned in the inscription, who gave birth to Denak (with the same name as her mother) and Shapur her brother, who succeeded Papak but was killed in an accident. Ardashir must have married a certain Mirdut, for she is identified as Shapur's mother, but is not given a title. This implies that she was not the principal wife of Ardashir, and perhaps only a concubine, not even married to him. Ardashir later may have married Denak, daughter of Papak from another wife, hence his half-sister, for she held the title Queen of Queens in the inscription.

The above suggests that Ardashir, like Darius the Achaemenid, had to prove his legitimacy and right to succeed Papak, but only in the inscription of his son Shapur do we find a hint of this.

Khoranzim, the Empire's Queen would be wife of Shapur King of Kings, while Aduranahid, Queen of Queens, is his daughter, according to the inscription.

3 Cf. Grignaschi 1966:49.

Parthian Culture and Costume

by Vesta Sarkhosh Curtis
BRITISH MUSEUM

The Parni or Aparni were nomads, who after establishing themselves around the River Ochus (modern Atrek), east of the Caspian Sea, under the leadership of Arsaces, a Scythian, invaded the former Achaemenid satrapy of Parthia and killed the Greek satrap Andragoras. This is what we learn about the Parthians from Strabo of the late first century BC–early first century AD and Justinus who was writing in the third century AD. Much is written about the unreliability of these secondary sources, but unfortunately we have no other information about the origin of the Parthians. Later Persian and Islamic writers had such a low opinion of the Parthians – and we shall discuss the reasons for this later – that they provide very little information about them, and most of this is inaccurate and unusable. The best source for early Parthian history is in fact Parthian coins (Wroth 1903; Sellwood 1980), and in addition these coins also give important information about Parthian material culture.

Most Parthian coins depict on the obverse the head of a ruler in profile and on the reverse a seated archer dressed in the Iranian fashion with long trousers and a long-sleeved coat slung over the shoulders. The legend on these coins is in Greek and all Parthian kings until the beginning of the first century AD only use the dynastic name Arsaces – hence the name Arsacids. The earliest Parthian coins show the ruler with a soft hat, perhaps made of felt, with a diadem tied around it (Pl. 1a). It is generally believed that, as in the Achaemenid period, only satraps or governors wore this type of headdress which indicates that at the time of Arsaces I and II the Parthians had not yet gained full independence and were still under the yoke of the Seleucids (Sherwin-White and Kuhrt 1993:89–90). It was not until the second century BC that the Parthians succeeded in shaking off the Seleucid yoke, and this major change is reflected in the coinage of Mithradates I (171–138/7 BC). Drachms of Mithradates I probably minted at the early Parthian capital of Nisa in modern Turkmenistan also show him with the so-called satrap's hat, but the legends on the reverse change from 'Arsaces' to 'the king Arsaces', and then to 'the great king Arsaces' (Pl. 1b-c). On later drachms from the mints of Nisa, Hecatompylos (Shahr-i Qumis in Damghan), and Ecbatana (modern Hamadan), the king's image changes and Mithradates is shown like a Seleucid king , wearing a Greek diadem which is the symbol of kingship (Pl. 1d).

During the reign of Mithradates I, Iran and Mesopotamia came under Parthian control. For strategic and economic reasons it was vital to have control over Mesopotamia, the fertile land between the rivers Tigris and Euphrates, and the growing sea trade with India via the Persian Gulf. Also, geographically Mesopotamia was closer to the western part of the Seleucid empire and later its successor, the Roman empire. Mithradates was crowned in the Greek city of Seleucia on the Tigris in 141 BC and he issued tetradrachms here which show him bearded and wearing the Greek diadem (Pl. 1e). The Greek legend describes him as ' the great king Arsaces, the philhellene'. The phrase 'philhellene', the Greek headband, and the apparently Greek dress all point to Greek influence at the Parthian court in the second century BC. Having wrested power from the Greek Seleucids, Mithradates was probably keen to depict himself in the Greek fashion. Perhaps he was also dependent on the support of the Greek ruling class in cities such as Seleucia or Susa and therefore proclaimed himself as 'philhellene', a title which remained popular until the time of Artabanus II (*c.*AD 10–38). The conquest of Mesopotamia was by no means a swift operation and cuneiform tablets tell of periods of unrest and at times the loss of Parthian control in southern Mesopotamia. In Elymais in southwestern Iran the local king, Kamnaskires I, staged a succesful but short revolt and issued his own coins in 147 BC. The revolt was soon crushed and Parthian supremacy was once again established at Susa when coins of Mithradates I were issued here in 140 BC.

Apart from coins, the art of the early Parthian period is mostly known from the fortress at Old Nisa, the first Parthian capital. Here at Mithradatkirt – the name is known to us from the many inscribed sherds or ostraca found – were discovered marble statuettes and delicate ivory rhytons (Pl. 2) which probably served as ritual drinking vessels, all dating to the second and first centuries BC. These objects have been fully published by the Russian scholars Mikhail Masson and Galina Pugachenkova (1956). The essentially Hellenistic style of the objects has been noted by many scholars (e.g. Invernizzi 1994). The mythological scenes decorating the upper friezes of the ivory vessels are clearly Greek in origin and the nude and semi-draped marble statuettes are made in the Hellenistic tradition. Fragments of painted clay statues (Col. Pl. I) and wallpaintings recently discovered by the Russian archaeologist Victor Pilipko (1991) are again largely Hellenistic in style but there there are also Iranian features in that the paintings show figures wearing trousers.

The architecture of Nisa is also largely Greek in inspiration but there may have been a type of *ivan* structure near the square Hall (Gabutti-Roncalli 1996: 166). It is possible that at nearby Mansur Tepe, about 3 kilometres north of Nisa, there is stronger evidence for Iranian influence in the early Parthian period. Here, there is a building with two *ivans* or vaulted chambers opening into a central courtyard. The problem is that Mansur Tepe is poorly dated, with bracket dates of second century BC until second century AD being suggested by the excavators (Koshelenko, Lapshin and Novikov 1989: 46). It is therefore not certain that we have here the remains of perhaps the earliest *ivan* structure.

From the end of the second century BC the image of the ruler on Parthian coins undergoes some change which is obviously of great significance. Artabanus I, still wearing the Greek diadem, is now shown with an upper garment that is open-necked and elaborately decorated (Pl. 1f). From now on the Parthian king wears an Iranian outfit which consists of jacket and trousers. The originally nomadic costume of the Parthians has replaced the ceremonial Greek dress. Increasing Iranian influence is clearly shown on the coins of Mithradates II (123–88/7 BC) (Pl. 1g-i), whose empire stretched from the Euphrates in the west to Bactria in the east. The king, who still describes himself as a philhellene, introduces a new upright hat as a sign of kingship and calls himself 'Arsaces, the great King of Kings, the beneficient'. The title king of kings was common amongst Assyrian and Achaemenid kings, and in the Parthian period also appears on cuneiform tablets from around 109 BC onwards.

Politically and geographically, the Parthian empire reached its peak and maximum extent at this time. Mithradates' campaign against the kingdom of Characene at the head of the Persian Gulf proved successful and bronze tetradrachms of Hyspaosines were overstruck with a portrait of Mithradates. In addition, a large part of northern Mesopotamia, including the city of Dura Europos, was conquered, probably in 113 BC. It was also at this time that Parthia and Rome began to quarrel over Armenia, which was the start of a long-standing conflict. By now Rome had become the successor to the Seleucid empire, while Parthia was in control of the overland trade routes and in particular the Silk Road. Control of Mesopotamia placed the Parthians in a strategically important position and enabled them to control the overland trade routes to China; they were now a serious threat to the Roman Empire. Probably from the time of Mithradates II is a rectangular relief set below the Achaemenid relief of Darius at Bisitun near Kermanshah (Fig. 7). The relief was badly

7 Seventeenth-century drawing of Parthian rock relief at Bisitun.

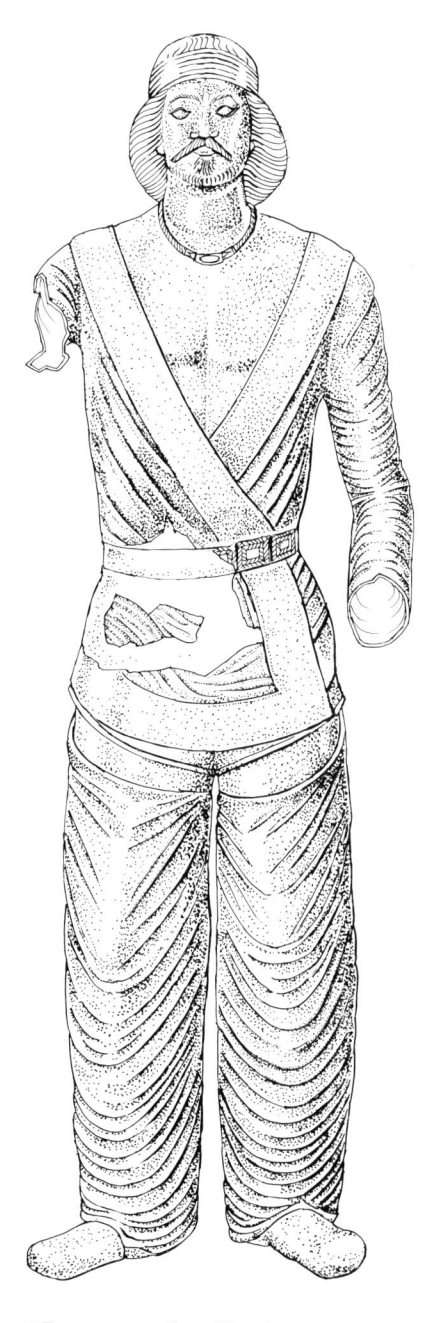

8 Bronze statue from Shami.

destroyed by an eighteenth-century inscription, but present evidence and a seventeenth-century sketch show what seems to have been a row of five standing men in profile. A Greek inscription carved above the panel mentions the personal name of Mithradates and his title 'great king' (Herzfeld 1920: 35–7, fig.11). The scene may show the satrap Gotarzes paying homage to Mithradates. Unfortunately, not much can be said about the costumes of the figures, as they are so badly preserved.

A distinct Parthian style, different from Greek artistic work as known from Nisa, for example, is finally developed by the end of the first century BC. This can be seen in the large bronze statue originally found in a temple at Shami in the Bakhtiari region (Fig. 8). This statue measures 1.90 metres in height and is now in the Muzeh Melli in Tehran. It was made in two parts, with the much smaller head being manufactured separately (Stein 1940; 131–2, pl. 146; Curtis, V.S., 1993a: 63–5). The bearded and moustached figure stands upright, facing front. He is clad in a short belted jacket with a V-shaped opening. A belt made of plaques, probably of metal and decorated with geometric motifs, holds the jacket together. Short trousers are worn under the jacket and tube-shaped leggings or over trousers cover the legs, leaving part of the upper thigh bare. The back of the statue shows how the leggings covered the backs of the thighs and then disappeared under the jacket, where they were probably attached to a hidden suspender belt. A cushion-type support which perhaps served for protection and comfort while riding appears at the back. Daggers are worn on the left and right sides with the hilts sticking out of the leggings. The figure has a long thin moustache and finely modelled beard. The tripartite hairstyle is rounded at the sides and a ridged diadem, the ties of which are no longer preserved, is tied across the forehead. He wears earrings and a torque with herringbone pattern and a central stone. The Shami figure with his short jacket and leggings and diadem and torque is paralleled on Parthian coins from the middle of the first century BC until the first century AD but the closest similarity is to coins of Phraates IV (Pl. 1j) whose tetradrachms show on the reverse a trouser-suit with wide lapels, a belt made up of metal plaques, leggings and even a dagger sticking out of the trousers. In fact, the Shami bronze provides the best example of a male figure appearing in the same way as on Parthian coinage.

From Parthian-period Susa comes a fragment of a small marble statue, now on display in the Muzeh Melli in Tehran, which could be a small replica of the Shami bronze (Pl.3; see also Curtis, V.S., 1993a: 63–4, fig.2, pl. XIX b-d). Clearly visible on the torso are a short jacket with wide lapels and a wide hem, a square indicating a belt plaque, and wide leggings.

Comparable with both the Shami bronze figure and the Susa statuette is the representation on a limestone stela from Ashur, one of a group of three, that is now in the Archaeological Museum in Istanbul (Pl. 4). It is assumed to have originated from the Parthian palace. The stela shows a bearded male figure with short hair standing frontally. He wears a short V-necked and belted jacket with broad lapels over short trousers and wide leggings, as on the Shami bronze, were probably attached to hidden suspenders. The symbols of the moon and the sun appear to the right of the head, while there is an illegible Aramaic inscription on the left side. An Aramaic inscription on one of the other stelae, no. III, has a date which according to Basil Aggoula's reading corresponds to AD 12/13 (Aggoula 1985: 26–8).[1] The same date may be suggested for Stela III as all three stelae, which had a commemorative purpose, must have been carved at the same time (Curtis, V.S., 1993a: 65–6).

Another example of a trouser-suit can be found on an eroded relief at Sar-i Pol-i Zohab on the main Baghdad-Kermanshah highway in western Iran. It shows a mounted figure in profile facing a standing male figure in frontal pose. Despite the bad condition of the relief it is possible to recognise certain details such as the diadem ties of the mounted figure, and it looks as if he may be holding a ring in his right hand. The standing figure, whose head is no longer preserved, wears a short belted jacket with a V-neck and leggings with diagonal folds. Of the Parthian inscriptions placed between the heads of the two figures and on both sides of the relief, only one, that on the left side, is legible and mentions that this was the image of 'the great king Gotarzes, son of the great king Giv' (Gropp 1968: 318; Trümpelmann 1977: 16). Historically there are two Parthian rulers named Gotarzes (Gudarz): one was a rival king to Mithradates II who is mentioned in Babylonian tablets of 91 BC and the other Gotarzes ruled from AD 38–51(see also the Bisitun relief). If we interpret the relief at Sar-i Pol as a royal relief then it must have been commissioned by Gotarzes II. Also, it is only in the first century AD that the Parthian script is used, as evidenced by coins of this time, for example those of Vologases I (AD 51–78). It is interesting to note that in the heroic section of Firdowsi's *Shahnameh* one of the principal heroes and allies of Rustam was Giv, the son of the *pahlavan* Gudarz /Gotarzes (Curtis, V.S., 1993b: 56).

Similar problems surround a jousting relief from Bisitun where hardly any details are visible. It is set to the right of the Mithradates relief that we have described above. It shows a combat scene involving two mounted knights with levelled spears with a mounted page at the left and a winged victory floating above the victorious central figure. Above the head of this central figure a Greek inscription gives the name 'Gotarzes Geopothros', which Herzfeld suggested (1932: 59–60) should not be read as 'Gotarzes, the son of Giv' but as 'Gotarzes Givputhr', Givputhr being a family name like the well-known Parthian families of the Suren, Karen and Mehran. However that may be, Malcolm Colledge has suggested (1977: 90–91) that this relief probably shows the historic battle between Gotarzes II and his rival Meherdates in AD 49–50.

The interpretation of the jousting scene at Bisitun as a battle between the Parthian King of Kings and a pretender is a clear indication of internal difficulties at this time. Increasing rivalries between claimants to the throne began to undermine central authority. It was during this time that one of the longest internal revolts occurred at Seleucia on the Tigris. It lasted from AD 36 until AD 43 during the rule of Artabanus II (Debevoise 1969: 164). Coinciding with the decrease in central power there was a marked increase in local artistic activity. The development and floruit of artistic movements in the late first – early third centuries AD has been best analysed by Edward Keall (1975: 627–32). He has pointed out that in the middle and late Parthian periods there was a decline in central power which resulted in the flourishing economy being no longer under the control of the Parthian king or the nobility. Instead, local merchants and robber barons profited from the thriving trade of luxury goods and spices from China and India to the the Eastern Roman empire. Keall goes so far as to suggest that it was the so-called *nouveaux riches* who acted as patrons of the arts and commissioned sculpture and buildings in the late Parthian period. An example of this new social trend may be the fortress known as Qaleh-i Yazdigird, in the remote Zagros mountains near Sar-i Pol-i Zohab in northwestern Iran, that flourished in the second century AD. The surface find of a coin of Mithradates IV of *c.* AD 140 at Qaleh-i Yazdigird supports this late date (Vollmer, Keall and Nagai-Berthrong 1983: 44). The whole stronghold covered an area of 25 square kilometres and from the Upper Castle it was possible to control the trade route and defend against enemies. Keall's excavations in the 1970s revealed traces of a so-called Palace or Royal Pavilion with a plan of three large halls surrounded by corridors that seems to resemble the plan of the north *ivan* of the Parthian palace at Ashur in northern Mesopotamia probably also of the second century AD (Keall 1982: 64, fig. 12). Furthermore, there is a striking resemblance between the stucco decoration on the Royal Pavilion at Qaleh-i Yazdigird and the elaborate geometric and floral plaster decoration on the facade of the late Parthian palace at Ashur (Andrae and Lenzen 1933: pl.14). The stucco decoration from Qaleh-i Yazdigird is of great importance (Vollmer, Keall and Nagai-Berthrong 1983: 40–3). It depicts female and male figures in the nude and semi-nude, heraldic animals and floral designs, and there is a plaque showing a frontal bust of a male figure with a typical tripartite hairstyle and headband. On a fragment of engaged column decorated with two square panels there is a standing female figure in the nude and a male figure standing frontally. The costume of the male figure (Pl. 5) consists of a tall pointed hat with earflaps and neckguard, a short belted tunic and trousers. The background and the scroll border were painted with yellow, ochre and blue, and blue was also used for the male figure himself. Of particular interest is a column capital painted in red showing a nude female figure holding the tails of dolphins (Herrmann 1977 : 72, pl. top left). Such engaged column capitals decorated with female figures, probably deities, are also known from other Parthian sites such as Merv in Turkmenistan, and Seleucia on the Tigris and Warka in southern Mesopotamia of the second century AD. The strong cultural links between Mesopotamia and the highlands of Iran are clearly demonstrated by the material culture of Qaleh-i Yazdigird.

It is precisely at this time that evidence for Parthian activity at sites in Mesopotamia is at its peak. For example, Seleucia (modern Tell Umar), an essentially Greek foundation by Seleucus I on the east bank of the river Tigris, and the centre of power and administration with its own mint, showed signs of a so-called Orientalisation after the revolt of the city in AD 36–44. Although occupation at many Mesopotamian sites continued uninterrupted after the arrival of the Parthians, not until the first-second century AD was there evidence for substantial building activity. Keall (1975: 625–7, 632) has suggested this was because Babylonian cities such as Babylon, Nippur and Warka were now profiting from the long-distance trade between East and West.

At Nippur, as at Seleucia, we see the gradual development of the *ivan*. As I mentioned above, the *ivan* is a vaulted hall which opens into a large courtyard, also known as *pīshgām*. This feature is also found in Sasanian architecture, most famously at Ctesiphon, and later becomes a standard element in Islamic mosques (Keall 1974: 125–8).

Babylon was an important centre in the Seleucid period and remained so into Parthian times. The Greek theatre which had been built in the Seleucid period was still in use at the end of the second century BC, as attested by winners' lists of *c*. 109 BC that record competitions that took place there, and dating from the Parthian period are many private houses and graves. In many cases the Babylonian house plan consisting of rooms grouped around a central courtyard is still found, but at a later date we find the introduction of a peristyle courtyard with columns (Koldewey 1914: 216–17, fig.131).

At Warka from the Parthian period there are ruins of temples, houses and a large number of graves, and written documents suggest that at the time of Mithradates II (123–88/7 BC) temples such as the Irigal were still intact (Kessler 1984: 276). The most significant feature of one of the houses was a courtyard with two *ivans* on either side. Another Parthian house with a large central courtyard and *ivans* was called by Heinrich (1935: 30–1, pl.1) the 'Parthischer Palast'. Amongst the plaster decoration in this building was a column capital with a male figure emerging out of acanthus leaves (Pl. 6). Parthian burials at Warka show how some of the deceased were placed in glazed clay slipper sarcophagi with relief decoration showing male figures dressed in jackets and baggy trousers standing in frontal position. The hairstyle is typically Parthian, arranged in bunches at the sides (Col. Pl. II) (Schmidt 1972: 63–9, pls. 26–9).

The same sort of architectural development noted in Babylonia can also be found at

Ashur in northern Mesopotamia. A new Ashur Temple was constructed with an *ivan*, and the Parthian palace has a group of four *ivans* probably dating from the first and second centuries AD (Andrae and Lenzen 1933: pls.10–11). We have already discussed the limestone stelae from Ashur and there are also fragments of limestone statues and a drawing on a vase which depict male figures in elaborately decorated tunics and trousers, all of them standing in frontal pose (Andrae and Lenzen 1933: 109, fig. 46 and pl. 58e).

In fact, there are terracotta figurines showing the Parthian trouser-suit from a number of Mesopotamian sites (Pl. 7), alongside figures shown in the nude or semi nude or shown wearing Greek dress (Ziegler 1962: pls. 27–9; Karvonen-Kannas 1995: pls. 58–61).

But undoubtedly the most elaborate examples of Parthian-style sculpture are known from Hatra (Safar and Mustafa 1974). The site lies 50 kilometres north of Ashur and over 100 kilometres southwest of Nineveh on the cross-desert route linking Palmyra and Dura Europos with Nineveh, Ashur and cities further east. Hatra therefore enjoyed a strategic position on an important trade route linking Mesopotamia with the west. The city may have been settled in the Seleucid period but there is no definite information until the end of the first century AD. By the end of the second century AD, Hatra was probably the capital of the province of Arabaya and may have had a mixed population of Arabs and Aramaeans. The exact status of the Hatrene kings is uncertain. On the one hand they call themselves 'king of the Arabs', demonstrating some political independence, but the fact that some kings adopted Parthian names, as for example Vorod, Valgash, that is Vologases, and Sinatruces may indicate some Parthian influence. Alternatively, this may simply reflect the fashion of the time. However, Hatra was probably not absorbed into the Parthian empire and its ascendancy may have coincided with the decline of the Parthian state, when it was weakened by internal quarrels and its treasury was exhausted by the numerous internal and external wars. It may have been convenient for the Parthians to allow Hatra some measure of independence, to keep a friendly buffer state between themselves and their Roman enemies. Also, it was beneficial to have a friendly state controlling the east-west trade route. The other petty states such as Edessa and Osroene were at times allies of Rome. In general, the political development of Hatra, with local kings ruling over the city but probably receiving their crown from the Parthian King of Kings, can be compared to Elymais and its relationship with Parthia. It is therefore natural that the art of Hatra reflects strong dependence on Parthian culture mixed with features that are local in origin. In addition, the lingering Hellenistic influence must not be ignored.

The architecture of Hatra is characterised by a series of both large and small *ivans*, and statues and reliefs of worshippers and their gods were found in many of the temples. The stone statues, although carved in the round, were only meant to be seen from the front, as the backs were roughly worked. Many male figures are dressed in tunic and trousers (Col. Pl. III). The tunic is sometimes short and plain or, more commonly, knee-length, belted and elaborately decorated. The baggy trousers are either plain or have elaborate decoration repeating that on the tunic. Sometimes there are vertical rows of discs. Combined with the trouser-suits there are sometimes over-garments. These include a shoulder cloak, a draped himation and occasionally also a long-sleeved coat left open in the front. Tall hats resembling the Parthian tiara and diadems with an eagle in the centre were both probably royal insignia. There is a wide range of belts: these can be plain, double looped or highly elaborate. The last sometimes consists of medallions decorated with figural busts, while other types are made up of plaques with geometric motifs and animal designs showing hares, kneeling ibexes and griffins.

Actual examples of such belt plaques have survived from Iran and Central Asia, but they are mostly unprovenanced. They are made of cast bronze and have openwork decoration showing embracing couples, rider figures, animals and so on. A circular gold belt clasp in the British Museum is allegedly from the Nahavand area (Pl. 8).

At Hatra, in some cases the type of belt and its decoration on inscribed and datable statues can be used to suggest dates for other pieces which are undated. For example the undated so-called Atalu statue (Pl. 9) wears a belt decorated with kneeling griffins which can be compared with the kneeling ibexes on the belt of King Sanatruq II, who ruled until AD 238. Therefore, the Atalu statue is probably of similar date. Furthermore, the tall hat of the Atalu statue is similar to tiaras on coins of the last two Parthian kings, Vologases VI and Artabanus IV, at the beginning of the third century AD (Pl. 1k). As well as on coins, Artabanus is depicted with a tall hat with spiky comb pattern on a relief from Susa in south western Iran which is dated by a Pahlavi inscription to AD 215 (Pl. 10).

More evidence of Parthian-period sculpture showing figures in tunics and trousers and in the typically Parthian frontal pose is known from Elymais, the Bakhtiari region of south western Iran. Here, the local kings who had enjoyed a certain degree of independence since AD 75 when they issued their own coins (Augé et al. 1979: 426) commissioned rock carvings to immortalise themselves and also built two major sanctuaries at Masjid-i Solaiman and Bard-i Nishandeh. Dedicatory statues and reliefs were discovered by Roman Ghirshman on the large terraces at Masjid-i Solaiman and nearby Bard-i Nishandeh both inside and around the various temples (Ghirshman 1976). The dedicatory statues and reliefs from both sites show bearded and moustached figures in frontal pose wearing tunics and trousers which are often elaborately decorated with designs similar to those found at Ashur and Hatra. On an architectural relief depicting a sacrificing scene (Ghirshman 1976: pl. XIII, 3), one of the figures wears a twisted sash over the left shoulder. It is interesting to note that the twisted sash, which may have had a religious significance, was perhaps part of the traditional costume of Elymais. Elymaian coins from the first century BC clearly show that a separate piece of material was worn over the shoulder (Pl. 11). Altogether, the sculpture from Bard-i Nishandeh and Masjid-i Solaiman ties in well with late Parthian period material of the second and early third centuries AD[2] both from southern and western Iran as well as late Parthian material from Mesopotamia.

There are also many Parthian rock reliefs in Elymais which contain much information about late Parthian period art in southwestern Iran (Vanden Berghe and Schippmann 1985; Kawami 1987: pls.11–18; Matthiesen 1992). At Hung-i Nauruzi, Hung-i Kamalvand, Bid Zard, Shimbar (or Shirin Bahar) and Tang-i Sarvak there are reliefs showing investiture scenes, banquet scenes, combat scenes and religious scenes. The isolated rock at Tang-i Sarvak (Pl.11) brings together examples of these different types of composition which were carved on different faces of the rock. One of the reliefs at Tang-i Sarvak has a good example of the typical Elymaian trouser-suit which is worn by a sacrificing king/priest. Some new discoveries by the Iranian archaeologist Jafar Mehrkiyan (1997: 69–72 and Pl. XIV; Curtis, V.S., and Simpson 1997: 140–43) in the last few years are particularly interesting. The two reliefs are at Shaivand and Shirinow Movri near Izeh, Malamir. At Shaivand a cult scene shows oxen and male figures wearing the Parthian outfit and facing front. At Shirinow Movri there is an almost almost exact replica of the banquet scene at Tang-i Sarvak with a figure seated on a throne. Also new is the discovery of an inscribed stone relief from Bazuft near Izeh, published by Rasul Bashshah (Curtis, V.S., and Simpson 1997: 140). It was accidentally discovered during pipeline works by the National Iranian oil company and depicts a banquet scene with four reclining figures.

The problem with many of the rock reliefs from Elymais is that their weathered condition does not allow us to recognise many details. Also, the inscriptions which appear on some of them only mention the name of the local ruler and therefore they cannot be dated with precision. Although they are crude and of little artistic merit they contain important information about late Parthian-period art in southwestern Iran. We see figures with the tripartite Parthian hairstyle, moustache and beard, dressed in the Parthian trouser-suit and shown frontally. The kings of Elymais are shown in the same way on their coins (Pl. 1m).

Some of these features are evident at sites outside the boundaries of the Parthian empire, particularly those to the west, such as Palmyra and Dura Europos.

Palmyra or ancient Tadmor was a caravan city in the Syrian desert which enjoyed an important strategic position on the east-west trade route. It became particularly important after the collapse of the Seleucid empire and the emergence of Rome as a major power with an interest in controlling trade routes. Palmyra and its Aramaic speaking population became part of the Roman empire during the reign of the emperor Nero (Colledge 1976: 17). When in the early third century AD trade was channelled through north Mesopotamian centres such as Edessa and Nisibis this had disastrous results for Palmyra and its merchants. The sculpture from Palmyra reflects the prosperity of the city's inhabitants before this time. Funerary busts and reliefs, which were representations of the dead people, were placed in underground tombs and tomb towers. Numerous representations of male figures in trouser-suits were found in temples as well as tombs, and gods worshipped at Palmyra were sometimes also shown wearing the Parthian trousers (Pl. 11). Inscriptions naming the deceased or the date of the construction of the buildings have been a great help with the dating of Palmyrene sculpture, showing that examples of tunics and trousers begin in the first century AD and continue until the first half of the third century AD. At Palmyra we find both Parthian frontality as well as many items of the Parthian costume.

The sheer number of reliefs depicting male figures in frontal pose wearing the Parthian costume (Colledge 1976) indicates the popularity of this type of outfit at Palmyra. The fact that figures are shown wearing the Parthian costume does not necessarily mean that the

9 Wall painting at Dura Europos showing figures in Parthian dress.

inhabitants of Palmyra really wore trousers, but the finding of textile fragments which have been identified as trousers with elaborate woven designs supports the idea that they actually did.

Elsewhere in Mesopotamia, a similar picture exists. At Roman Dura Europos on the west bank of the Euphrates, many examples of the Parthian costume can be seen in the wall paintings of the Synagogue, the Mithraeum, the Temple of the Palmyrene Gods and many other temples and also private houses (Fig. 9; Kraeling 1956; Perkins 1973; Downey 1977). Graffiti from some of the private houses show scenes that include a galloping horseman in Parthian hairstyle and dress, a mounted warrior in chain mail, and a seated king (Cumont 1926, Perkins 1973). While Palmyra was never under Parthian control, Dura was probably occupied by the forces of Mithradates II in 113 BC and the city became one of the western frontier posts of the Parthian empire until AD 165 when it came permanently under Roman control. Tomb mosaics from Edessa in northern Mesopotamia also depict rows of figures in Parthian frontal pose and the Parthian costume (Colledge 1977: pl. 47a) and coins of Gordian III and Abgar, king of Edessa in the third century AD, show Abgar with the Parthian tiara, a belted tunic and trousers (Pl. 1n-o).

I hope I have been able to demonstrate that it is possible to identify certain features that are characteristic of Parthian material culture, namely the *ivan* architecture, the Parthian hairstyle and costume and frontality in art. These can be identified over a large and diverse geographical area, including Iran and Mesopotamia, which was controlled by the Parthians for 400 years. The Parthians certainly did not invent the trouser-suit, as this was already worn in the Achaemenid period by a number of Iranian peoples who shared an originally tribal background and were horse-riders. The Iranian delegations on the Apadana reliefs at Persepolis including the delegations from the Achaemenid satrapies of Parthia and Bactria (Delegations XIII and XV) all wore trousers and amongst these the Medes, Scythians and Sargatians (Delegations I, XI and XVI) bring trousers as tribute to the Achaemenid king. The gold plaques of the Achaemenid-period Oxus Treasure show figures who wear knee-length tunics and trousers with a long-sleeved coat slung over the shoulders (Dalton

1964) and Scythian art of the fifth to the fourth centuries BC depicts male figures in jackets and trousers (Artamonov 1969). The achievement of the Parthian kings was to make the trouser-suit the official ceremonial costume. In official Achaemenid court art the kings are always portrayed wearing long Oriental dresses. We saw that coins of Artabanus I in the second century BC show the king wearing a jacket as part of the trouser-suit, and this type of costume was worn by all his successors, who made it popular in the ancient Near East. The fashion of the time was also adopted by the Iranian Kushans in Bactria whose coins and statues show the king and worshipping figures with a knee-length tunic and trousers. The Iranian revival was an achievement of the Parthian Arsacids who although they claimed to be philhellenes and also imitated the Greek artistic style for at least 200 years, nevertheless succeeded in leaving a strong Iranian imprint on the cultures of the areas under their rule and adjacent areas.

Unfortunately, little credit has been given to the Parthians either by modern scholars or by ancient writers. Firdowsi, for example, who devoted some 55,000 double verses to the mythology of ancient Iran and the history of the Sasanians, describes the Parthian period in only 20 double verses and claims that he did not find anything about them in the *Shahnameh* or Book of Kings, although unknown to Firdowsi he had incorporated many heroic stories of the Parthian *pahlavans* Giv, Gudarz, Gorgin and Bijan and even Rustam in his heroic section. The Sasanian propaganda machine succeeded in eliminating traces of the Parthians and their 400 years of rule. In actual fact, though, they inherited much from the Parthians. When Ardashir I defeated Artabanus (Ardavan) in AD 224 his first coins show him with the tiara of Mithradates II (Pl. 12a). He and his successors also continued to wear the Parthian trouser-suit as their ceremonial outfit. It was actually the Parthians who re-introduced Iranian elements into post-Hellenistic Iran rather than the Sasanians, but it was the latter who went down in history as the true successors of the Achaemenids and the dynasty that revived Iranian art and culture.

Notes

1 A new reading of the inscription by Klaus Beyer (1998: 11, no. A4) suggests a date of 112–13 AD, but on stylistic grounds an earlier date is perhaps to be preferred.

2 The prosperity of Elymais in the second century AD is shown by the finds from the cemetery at Gelalak south of Shushtar, recently discovered by Mehdi Rahbar (Curtis, V.S., and Simpson 1998: 189–90).

The Rock Reliefs of Sasanian Iran[1]

by Georgina Herrmann
UNIVERSITY COLLEGE, LONDON

It is a remarkable concept to choose a cliff and carve a sculpture on it, a sculpture which in most cases will be dwarfed by its setting. Yet such reliefs, which are quite different from 'rock art', have been carved for millennia. In Iran the tradition of rock relief began in the late third or the early second millennium BC, with reliefs of the kings of the Lullubi and of the Elamite kings (Vanden Berghe 1959, 1983). A magnificently sited example at Kurangun is an outstanding example of an Elamite rock relief, and one of importance because it illustrates the long-term significance of the site to the Elamites: the central scene was carved in the second millennium BC, while the worshippers were added in the first (Vanden Berghe 1983: fig. 2, and pl. 3). This continuity is a major factor in the siting of many reliefs: at Naqsh-i Rustam near Persepolis, for instance, there are reliefs of the Elamite kings, the well-known Achaemenian tombs with their sculptured facades, as well as Sasanian and post-Sasanian reliefs (Fig. 10; Vanden Berghe 1983: pl. 7; Curtis, J.E., 1989: fig. 46). There are also other features in the vicinity, the well-known Ka'bah-i Zardusht, the Sasanian fire-altars, exposure platforms for the dead and so on, as well as the nearby Naqsh-i Rajab grotto and city of Istakhr.

Rock relief in Iran was only sporadically employed as an art form. After the Elamites a famous example from the first millennium BC was the monumental sculpture and trilingual inscription of Darius I carved at Bisitun, near Kermanshah (Vanden Berghe 1983: pl. 6; Curtis, J.E., 1989: fig. 44). This victory relief commemorated his reconquest of empire. There were only a few rather indifferent reliefs of the Seleucid and Parthian kings, until the late Parthian period when the rulers of the vassal kingdom of Elymais in southwestern Iran carved a lively range of motifs on large free-standing boulders (Vanden Berghe 1983: 38–53; Vanden Berghe and Schippmann 1985). Motifs on boulders in the Tang-i Sarvak valley show a ruler reclining indolently and holding up the ring of power, a huge figure

10 Sketch of the tombs and reliefs at Naqsh-i Rustam.

saluting an altar, rows of courtiers attending a seated figure and a mounted knight jousting with a lance (Vanden Berghe and Schippmann 1985: 59–88). In typical Parthian style, many of the figures are represented frontally. This flourishing and lively, if somewhat provincial school of sculpture is variously dated to the first two to three centuries AD. There is no reason to suppose that this art had anything to do with the Parthian ruling dynasty: it was almost certainly commissioned by local kings.

Like the Elymaians, Ardashir was a minor vassal king when he challenged and defeated his Parthian overlord, Artabanus IV, in about 224 AD, founding the Sasanian empire. This was to last for four centuries until overcome by the energy of a new religion, Islam. It may well have been the carvings of Elymais that inspired Ardashir to employ rock relief as an official art form. His sculptures initiated one of the most coherent and remarkable periods of rock relief art in Iran, one followed for some 60 years by his successors, nearly all of whom carved reliefs in the Sasanian homeland of Fars. Of the total of some 34–5 reliefs of the Sasanian period, the majority, some 28 in all, are in Fars. Most of these are concentrated on only three sites, two near Persepolis (Naqsh-i Rustam and Naqsh-i Rajab) and one at Bishapur, and can be dated to the third and early fourth centuries AD. The sequence of reliefs then comes to an end. There are no reliefs that can certainly be attributed to Shapur II (AD 309–79), who reigned for 70 years during the greater part of the fourth century. The three post-Shapur Sasanian reliefs were all carved in a hunting park or 'paradise' at Taq-i Bustan near the great east-west highway which linked Ctesiphon with Khurasan and the east. Reasons for this change may be that the focus of empire had shifted to Ctesiphon and Khuzistan. Thereafter, no more rock reliefs were carved in Iran until the nineteenth century when the Qajar kings, fascinated by the Achaemenians and Sasanians, revived both rock reliefs and bas reliefs decorating buildings.

When Ardashir became King of Kings he had to grapple with the problem facing all such new dynasts. Power – kingship – has to be visible, whenever and wherever it exists. Ardashir wanted to represent his new status in a distinctive manner, which, although it could and did draw on earlier Iranian and Mesopotamian traditions, had to be instantly recognisable. We rarely have the opportunity to observe a ruler's groping for a satisfactory visual language: we are usually presented with the *fait accompli*. For instance, what we think of as Achaemenid iconography is essentially not that of Cyrus the founder, of whom we know little in symbolic terms, but that of Darius, the administrator. It is with Darius at Susa and Persepolis that we see the developed Achaemenid art that symbolised that dynasty (Roaf 1989).

We are more fortunate with the art of the Sasanians, for a distinctive visual language was established by Ardashir. The evolution of this language can be traced on both his superb coinage (Pl. 12) and his rock reliefs. The coins offer the longer sequence, and on them we can trace changes from when he was a vassal of the Parthians to the last years of his reign when his son Shapur joined him in ruling the empire. The earliest type (Pl. 12a) shows him as a sub-king of his father Papak, himself vassal ruler of Istakhr near Persepolis. Both wear the Parthian high hat with ear and neck flaps: Papak is represented frontally in typical Parthian style, while Ardashir faces to the left (Göbl 1971: pl. 1, nos. 1–2). On his seizure of power Ardashir faces the opposite direction in what was to become the standard Sasanian manner, and on the reverse we see the motif of the fire altar (Pl. 12b) (Göbl 1971: pl. 1, nos. 4–8).

The third type (Pl.12c) depicts Ardashir wearing a rather remarkable crown, formed by dividing his hair into two and pulling some curls up into a topknot with the rest falling on the neck (Göbl 1971: pl. 1, no. 16). The top-knot was then covered to form a high globe or *korymbos*, an element represented on all except the latest Sasanian crowns (Göbl 1971: pl. 1, nos. 9–11). This crown became his personal crown. Successive Sasanian kings also developed their own distinctive crowns, the different types of which were first established from the coinage in the 1930s by Ernst Herzfeld. It was the wearing of such personal crowns that has often made possible the identification of kings illustrated on rock reliefs, silver bowls or stuccoes. However, nothing in life is that simple: although the general principle is accepted, and many sound identifications have been made, there are frequently disputes. It is not my intention to discuss such problems here.

Ardashir's coins are themselves works of art. Because of their widespread distribution, coins were one of the most effective forms of publicity, the mass media of the day if one thinks in those terms. The standardised images were minted in cities throughout the empire, on bronze issues as well as the more glamorous gold and silver. Such coins visually served to emphasise the change of power.

Just as we can observe the successive stages in the development of a distinctive image on Ardashir's coins, so also can we watch his striving for a sculptural style to advertise his newly-won power on a monumental scale. This took time, for Vladimir Lukonin, in whose honour this seminar is held, suggested that coins with his personal crown were not minted until the early 230s, and this crown is shown on even his earliest relief (Lukonin 1968). So Ardashir's sculptural development must have been concentrated in less than a decade, for he had handed over power to his son Shapur by the end of that decade.

His earliest relief was carved in the narrow gorge which leads to the plain of Firuzabad, where he built his new city, known as Ardashir Khurrah or the Glory of Ardashir. This relief is simple in design and technique, with little improvement on Elymaian reliefs: the god Ahuramazda or Ohrmazd hands Ardashir the ribboned diadem, the symbol of kingship (Vanden Berghe 1983: pl. 17). Behind him stands his son and successor Shapur, identified by the device on his hat. Such heraldic devices or 'family crests' enable us to identify a number of Sasanian members of the royal family and major families. The message is political: Ardashir is legitimising his seizure of power by illustrating his divine investiture with the right to rule, the royal *farr*, an almost mystical manifestation without which it was not possible to reign in Iran.

In his second relief, Ardashir commemorated his seizure of power by illustrating the moment of victory in a vivid series of contests. Three Sasanian knights overcome three Parthian warriors in separate single combats – the highest form of warfare in ancient Iran. The first pair can be identified as Ardashir (Pl. 13), overwhelming the Parthian king, the second is Shapur defeating the Parthian Grand Vizier, while the third is the fan-bearer from the investiture scene, who is sweeping a third Parthian off his horse. Identification of the figures is made possible by the heraldic devices worn both on their hats and on the caparisons of the horses.

Some scholars have thought the Firuzabad jousting scene to be of poor quality – little more than a crude drawing in stone (Ghirshman 1962: 126). Part of the reason may be that it is extremely difficult to see. The relief is carved near the top of the mountain beside an old road which has long since disintegrated. It is only lit for a brief period by the sun as it rises, after which, when in shade, it is almost impossible to locate, especially from the modern road at the bottom of the valley. Even when you have climbed the mountain it is hard to see, for the scene is high above the current ground surface. It is difficult to make out details and even harder to photograph. With the benefit of a ladder, however, it immediately becomes evident how superbly the piece was carved and how dynamic the design. Although the depth of relief is relatively shallow, the modelling is excellent and the finished surface finely worked and polished. The design itself is rather reminiscent of a painting by Stubbs, with the horses depicted in a flying gallop. And everything else contributes to the feeling of movement with ribbons and the extraordinary balloon-like attachments flying up in the air. It is a unique work, and shows how Ardashir's sculptors were improving both in their vivid design and in their technique of carving.

Ardashir's relief at Naqsh-i Rustam near Persepolis combined both motifs recorded at

Firuzabad, investiture and victory, in a single scene (Col. Pl. V; Vanden Berghe 1993: pl. 59). I consider that this sculpture is the finest relief of the Sasanian period, but this is a matter of opinion, and one certainly not shared by the travel writer Robert Byron, who described all the carvings of Naqsh-i Rustam as 'negative art or repellent. But while the mountains last, the rock maniacs who commanded these things must be remembered – and they knew it' (Byron 1937: 179).

His Naqsh-i Rustam investiture illustrates Ardashir's success in developing a distinctive visual language suitable for reproduction on a large scale. Two horsemen exchange a diadem, the symbol of the right to rule. There is no doubt about their identification, not only because of their crowns but thanks to inscriptions carved on their horses. Their defeated enemies, the dead Parthian king and Ahriman, the spirit of evil, lie beside their horses' hooves. The scene was carved in high relief, practically in the round. The dramatic effect of the sculpted figures was enhanced by a high polish, set against a background which was deliberately left rough. Although this relief is static when compared with the jousting scene, nevertheless there is movement in the ribbons of the diadem and the god's fluttering cloak – a breeze is blowing from the king.

Ardashir handed over power to his son before he died, and Shapur I (AD 240–72), of course, recorded his own investiture in the nearby grotto of Naqsh-i Rajab, his personal crown resembling that of Ohrmazd. However, Shapur's principal sculptural theme was his remarkable success in decisively defeating the formidable Roman army, not once but at least four times. Two very different versions of these victories were carved on large panels, both similar in size, although from illustrations of them this is hard to believe. The one with only three figures is carved below the tombs of the Achaemenian kings at Naqsh-i Rustam (Vanden Berghe 1993: pl. 68), while the multi-register relief with more than 200 figures is carved in a gorge adjacent to Shapur's new city of Bishapur (Col. Pl. VI; Vanden Berghe 1993: pl. 76). All that the two monumental sculptures have in common is that they were commissioned by the same patron and illustrate the same subject.

Unfortunately, the Bishapur relief is poorly preserved: not only was it damaged by a water channel running along the bottom register, but also areas of the surface have flaked off. However, the essentials survive. The central register is the tallest and most important of the five, with the principal scene dramatised by leaving blank the areas above and below. To the left can be seen the mounted figure of the king, with his hand grasping that of a shadowy figure standing by the horse's hindquarters: a corpse lies beside his horse, while in front a pleading figure is on his knees. Remains of their dress indicate that these represent Romans.

In one of the few surviving royal inscriptions, which was carved on the Achaemenian tower at Naqsh-i Rustam, the Ka'bah-i Zardusht, Shapur described his Roman wars and his victories over the young Gordianus III, who died, Philip the Arab, who sued for peace, and the elderly Valerian, whom he captured with his own hand (Frye 1984: 371–3, Appendix 4). It is these triumphs which were recorded in this relief with the dead Gordian, the pleading Philip and Valerian whom he claimed to have 'captured by my own hand'. However, such a scene never took place: these victories did not occur in a single event, but in three separate campaigns taking place over 20 years. Sasanian reliefs are not trying to represent a 'real event', any more than Achaemenian sculptures were. Of the three Roman emperors only the captured Valerian could feasibly have been present. The reliefs are symbolic representations rather than any sort of photographic record.

Behind the king are registers of Sasanian knights, the armed might of the empire; in front are rows of tributaries bringing gifts. These are Romans and Iranians, probably from eastern Iran. Again the images are symbolic: they make manifest the king's power and the extent of his empire in a manner common from Assyrian times. The design is reminiscent of Achaemenian reliefs from Persepolis in the use of registers, in the balancing of Medes and Persians with tributaries, and in the bringing of gifts rather than illustrating victory by humiliation. While the general composition may reflect Achaemenian influence, the complexity of much of the design and the vitality of the carving suggests the employment of Roman sculptors, although sculptors working to a strict Sasanian brief. The use of Roman artisans is of course well known and illustrated by mosaics from the city of Bishapur, as well as the construction of complex barrages for water control at Dizful and Shushtar.

The Bishapur sculpture is a remarkable work of art, with a subtle and complex design and dynamic carving. Worked on a convex curve, the horses on the left seem almost to be prancing out of the stone (Pl. 14), while the Romans in the lowest register, with their backs turned, register the despair of defeat. However, in my view it fails to communicate its message clearly and is difficult to see from both near and far. Its 'failure' is evident if we contrast it with the Naqsh-i Rustam relief with its monumental figures (Col. Pl. VII; Vanden Berghe 1993: pl. 68). The message of Naqsh-i Rustam is unequivocal – and can be established readily from a distance – the Sasanian king triumphant over the Roman empire personified by the submissive figures of defeated emperors.

Most Sasanian rock reliefs were content with a single scene, and as such I have always considered them to be the equivalent of an advertisement hoarding. They present a relatively simple message on a large scale located in a reasonably public place with the aim of influencing passers-by. However, the simile may be simplistic, relying as it does on modern concepts of public media designed to influence opinion. For instance, advertisement hoardings are readily duplicated and designed to be seen by those passing by. A rock relief on the other hand is a 'one-off' design,[2] and there is doubt as to how accessible they were. Access to official art was restricted in many societies. For example the bas-reliefs decorating palaces at Persepolis or Nineveh could only be seen by the small part of the population with access to the royal palaces. So were rock reliefs generally accessible, or should we think about the possibility of controlled access?

Most Sasanian reliefs were located near cities. Eight were carved on the great cliff of Naqsh-i Rustam and four more in the grotto of Naqsh-i Rajab, near the city of Istakhr. Six reliefs were carved in the Bishapur gorge adjacent to Shapur's new city. Two more were carved beside the old road on the way to Ardashir's magnificent circular city at Firuzabad and one not far from his city of Darabgird. The remainder were scattered and often carved on less significant sites.

Certainly the earliest reliefs, those of Ardashir at Firuzabad, would have been visible to travellers on the old Sasanian road and may have been carved with public viewing in mind. However, access to those at Naqsh-i Rustam and Naqsh-i Rajab, close to Istakhr with its Temple of Anahita, may well have been restricted. Naqsh-i Rustam was an area of significance from Elamite times, and both Naqsh-i Rustam and the nearby grotto of Naqsh-i Rajab may have been enclosed. The accessibility of the Bishapur reliefs is more difficult to ascertain, for today a road runs through the gorge. Isolated reliefs, often close to water, may have been sited in gardens with restricted access, like the later reliefs at Taq-i Bustan, located in a Sasanian paradise. With controlled viewing of many reliefs I think we can assume that, as with the official decoration of palaces, the message was not intended for the general public but aimed at a restricted audience.

While accessibility is one aspect of interest, another is the light the reliefs may shed at an unintentional or subconscious level on events in Sasanian Iran. Because of the paucity of surviving records – these were usually written on perishable materials – the reliefs form one of the few sources to offer a glimpse into the king's mind. For instance, Ardashir's reliefs reflect his desire to legitimise his seizure of power, based on victory and sanctioned by divine authority, while for Shapur his primary message was the magnitude of his victories against Rome. However, the reliefs carved at the end of the third century tell a very different story and offer fascinating insights into the decline of royal power, the result, once again, of the power of the 'great families', a major destabilising aspect of Iranian society. They also document the power of one man, the long-lived priest Kartir (Hinz 1969: 189–228).

Kartir had begun his career under Ardashir and was still active in the reign of Narseh (AD 293–302). He became the real power behind the throne, a king-maker who probably ensured the succession of Shapur's grandson Bahram II (AD 276–93). Even at this distance in time, the extent of his power is demonstrated by his having his bust and inscription added to the big victory relief of Shapur I at Naqsh-i Rustam. In this case a private individual, even if an important one, had added his portrait to the official royal document of a major earlier king. In addition to his own busts and inscriptions, Kartir was also represented in all the reliefs of his protegé, Bahram II, except the first.

Bahram's first relief was carved at Bishapur in the style of his grandfather, Shapur I, and his father, Bahram I (Vanden Berghe 1983: pl. 25), the figures of the mounted kings in these reliefs being closely similar. This is the only one of Bahram's reliefs concerned with external affairs, and it shows the king receiving a foreign delegation (Vanden Berghe 1983: pl. 28). The subsequent emphasis on internal affairs is hardly surprising since Bahram's reign was 'wracked by civil war within and by heavy setbacks in his conflict against Rome, forcing the king to cooperate more closely with the aristocracy and clergy' (Wiesehöfer 1996: 213). Reliefs at Sarab-i Bahram and Naqsh-i Rustam (Vanden Berghe 1993: pls. 64–5) show Bahram flanked by members of the aristocracy, including of course Kartir, identified by the device or emblem on his hat (Pl. 15; Hinz 1969: pl. 121), as well as members of his family at Naqsh-i Rustam. Such scenes illustrate the king's preoccupation with internal affairs, with propitiating Kartir and appeasing power factions within the court. There is also an interest in ensuring the survival of his family, which is echoed on his coins and a silver dish (Harper and Meyers 1981: pl. 2).

Kartir's busts are unequivocal evidence that private individuals were allowed to commission reliefs during the reign of Bahram II. However, in my view – and I should stress here that this is my personal view and not one necessarily agreed with by other scholars – it was not only Kartir who commissioned reliefs at this time. The increasing power of the great families led to other non-official or 'private' reliefs, of which the most charming was carved on a free-standing boulder near a spring at Tang-i Qandil (Col. Pl. VIII; Vanden Berghe 1993: pl. 66). It may well have been set within a paradise, perhaps belonging to the Sasanian magnate who is offered a flower by his lady.[3]

Other non-official reliefs include a similar scene carved on rocks surrounding a pool at Barm-i Dilak near Shiraz, as well as single panels showing Bahram II and a high official there (Hinz 1969: pls.136–9). The standard of carving of the Barm-i Dilak reliefs is relatively poor, as it is on a panel showing the king carved on a rock in a modern garden at Guyum. None of these, in my view, belongs to central Sasanian royal production.

It was only after deposing Bahram's son and successor, Bahram III, that Narseh (AD 293–302), the last of Shapur's sons, succeeded to the throne. Not surprisingly he carved an investiture scene at Naqsh-i Rustam, where he was invested with royal authority by the goddess Anahita (Vanden Berghe 1993: pl. 60). During his reign, Iran suffered further reverses. The power of the great families continued to interfere with the succession and there were intrigues before the accession both of Hormuzd II (AD 302–9) and of Shapur II. Hormuzd II also carved a relief at Naqsh-i Rustam, a simplified version of Ardashir's jousting scene from Firuzabad, with the king unhorsing an unidentified opponent (Fig. 11; Overlaet 1993: pl. 77). Thereafter there are no certain *official* reliefs until the end of the

11 Jousting scene of Hormuzd II at Naqsh-i Rustam.

fourth century. Most significantly there is not one relief which can definitely be attributed to the long-lived Shapur II, a king who successfully restored Iran's fortunes in both the west and the east.

This absence of offical rock reliefs is in no way an indication that official art declined in the fourth century. Indeed, as Prudence Harper stated in her seminal study, *Silver Vessels of the Sasanian Period,* production was standardised with strict quality controls applied, thanks to 'the extraordinarily long occupation of the throne by Shapur II, and his unquestioned ability. . . . Shapur II established certain prerogatives for the monarchy, thereby curtailing the rights of both the nobility and clergy. . . . At a different level of society Shapur organised the artisans, separating the workers into corporations according to metier. Over all the artisans there was a chief, *kirrokbad*, appointed by the king. Posi, a Syrian, was at first chief of the court workers at Karkha de Ledan, becoming later chief of the artisans of other regions in the empire' (Harper and Meyers 1981: 17).

Similar controls may well have been applied to stucco decoration, as shown in the decoration of a Sasanian building excavated in the 1970s by Massoud Azarnoush at Hajiabad, not far from Darabgird in Fars (Azarnoush 1994). Azarnoush considered the building to be not a palace but the manor house of an important dignitary, and this is significant, for we are therefore looking at decoration commissioned by a major but not a royal personage. The decoration included two busts of the king, which, thanks to the individual crowns worn by the early Sasanian kings, can be identified as Shapur II. The presence of these royal busts indicated that representations of the monarch could and did form part of the decorative scheme of a private dwelling: the representation of a king on a rock relief as at Barm-i Dilak or Guyum need not, therefore, necessarily be a royal commission.

The royal busts are of two sizes, large and medium, and were prepared from moulds, as were all except two busts, which probably represented the owner and his son. It may be significant that the royal busts were moulded rather than carved, for we can be sure that in Shapur's Iran the right to represent the king would have been strictly controlled: those magnates who wished to demonstrate their loyalty by decorating their houses with busts of the king would have had to use approved moulds.

The controls imposed by Shapur II make it evident that the absence of rock reliefs during his reign was deliberate. This probably reflected both the decline in the importance of Fars and the increasing popularity of stucco decoration. Stucco had been favoured from the Hellenistic period. The mountain fortress of Qaleh-i Yazdigird of the late Parthian/early Sasanian period, excavated by E.J. Keall in the 1970s (Keall 1989: 52–4), presented a riotous display of brilliantly coloured and varied imagery. The corpus of known Sasanian stucco work at Kish, Ctesiphon and Hajiabad, as well as the recently discovered palace at Bandiyan in Khurasan (Curtis, V.S., and Simpson 1998: 186–7) make evident the widespread popularity of stucco (Kröger 1982).

Stuccoes were, of course, painted, and this brings me to another point. Although we may not be aware of it today, most ancient and medieval sculpture was not monochrome but highly coloured – whether it was an Assyrian or Achaemenian relief, the Parthenon sculptures or medieval sculptures. Indeed there is another fascinating avenue which we could explore in this lecture – the effect of the opinions of the eighteenth-century German art critic J.J. Winckelmann. He identified the 'highest ideals of art with classical Greek statues of young men in white marble', even when 'archaeologists were bringing forward evidence that ancient sculptors had employed colour by combining materials, as in the chryselephantine statue of Athena that once stood in the Parthenon, and by painting their statues and reliefs' (Lynton 1997: 6). Winckelmann's writ 'became law overnight for every high-minded artist, patron and art-lover'. It is only recently that scholars have begun to question this hypothesis and to emphasise that the Parthenon marbles – and other ancient sculptures – were once brilliantly coloured. So we need to look at Sasanian rock reliefs and Assyrian or Achaemenian sculptures with the realisation that originally they were painted. Obviously, little evidence survives today after centuries of weathering. However, fragments of plaster survive on at least two reliefs at Bishapur (Herrmann 1983: 12–13) and traces of colour have been recovered from the Persepolis sculptures. Just how brilliantly coloured these may have been has been suggested in a colour reconstruction of the symbol of Ahuramazda/Ohrmazd from Persepolis prepared by the Italian scholar A.B. Tilia (Roaf 1989: fig. 25).

The 'switch to stucco' of Shapur's reign had a profound effect on the later reliefs of the dynasty. These were located in a beautiful paradise where a mountain sweeps down to rich springs of water, at Taq-i Bustan near Kermanshah, a site strategically located near the main east-west highway linking Mesopotamia with Iran and the east. These sculptures are entirely different in style to the earlier Fars reliefs and seem to me to be stone versions of stucco originals. Significantly, two of them were actually set within an architectural frame, *ivans* carved out of the mountain (Herrmann 1989: pl. 23).

We will now focus on the magnificent final statement of the dynasty. Unfortunately the identity of the king is uncertain, for the crowns, our key at the beginning of the dynasty, are immensely elaborate but less distinctive. Most scholars, however, believe that the crown is probably that of Khusro II (AD 591–628). His accession was contested, and the king had to flee and appeal to the Byzantine emperor Maurice for assistance. From this uneasy beginning, he became a mighty conqueror, even seizing Jerusalem. In familiar mode the sculptures on the back wall illustrate his investiture and epitomise his conquests (Pl. 16; Vanden Berghe 1993: pl. 63). He is invested by both Ohrmazd and the goddess Anahita, while the magnificent figure of the king in full armour, lance at the ready, represented invincibility (Overlaet 1993: pl. 78). The scenes are themselves framed by the arch of the *ivan*, itself decorated with an untied diadem, winged victories and panels with stylised trees.

The scenes on the side walls show events that would have taken place in the paradise: on one wall is a stag hunt, on the other a boar hunt in the marshes (Vanden Berghe 1993: pls. 73–74). The whole is distinctly reminiscent of one of the lion hunts of the Assyrian king Ashurbanipal. In both, action takes place within the palisades enclosing the paradise and is shown in similar 'comic strip' form. All stages of the hunt are represented. Elephants flush the boar out of the reeds towards the royal party in their barges. Herds flee across the top of the picture and fill the left side of the scene. The king, the focal point of the scene, shoots a boar shown twice, first as it charges, all aggression with tail up, and then again defeated and dying. The king is shown a second time at rest, listening to the musicians in the accompanying boat. Beyond the palisade elephants bear away the dead boar, while others escape to be hunted another day.

As I have said, I consider the *ivan* and its decorative scheme to be a stone version of the elaborate stucco which once decorated Sasanian and early Islamic buildings, and parallels, although only fragmentary of course, can be found for all the elements: the scenes on the back wall, the hunts and other elements such as the diadem framing the arch of the iwan, the angels or Winged Victories in the spandrels and the stylised trees.[4]

The art of the Sasanian empire was widely disseminated throughout Asia and Europe thanks to designs on Sasanian silks, silver and stucco. Perhaps its very success and longevity lay in its apparent appeal to the senses and lack of an obvious political or religious message. Much of the imagery was dedicated to pleasure, with beautiful scenes of hunting and banqueting, of musicians and dancing ladies, as well as animal, floral and geometric motifs. As a rigidly controlled, official state art, this relative lack of message is surprising, especially in an empire with an orthodox state religion and one constantly at war. It may be, however, that we fail to understand the subtlety of the visual language. With its roots deep in Mesopotamian iconography, the Taq-i Bustan *ivan* can be seen as a Sasanian version of the standard Assyrian or Mesopotamian view of monarchy: the king was the 'chosen of the gods', 'crowned with splendour', 'fearless in battle' and a hero at war and the hunt (Grayson 1976: 120–1). The very same range of designs as in Ashurnasirpal's throne room at Nimrud occur more than a millennium later at Taq-i Bustan – divine investiture, victory, the hunt and the long-lived stylised tree. In fact, let us end with the wonderful words of Ashurnasirpal II (883–859 BC):

> 'At that time my sovereignty, my dominion (and) my power came forth at the command of the great gods; I am king, I am lord, I am praise-worthy, I am exalted, I am important, I am magnificent, I am foremost, I am a hero, I am a warrior, I am a lion, and I am virile. . .' (Grayson 1976:121).

Notes

1 I am very grateful to Michael Roaf for reading an early version of this paper and making many helpful comments.
2 Smaller clay versions of some reliefs might have been more widely distributed, as Ursula Seidl recently established for the Darius relief at Bisitun.
3 Vanden Berghe considered that Bahram II is illustrated both at Tang-i Qandil and Barm-i Dilak (1993:80). For another view of the date and interpretation of this and other Sasanian reliefs, see Levit-Tawil 1993.
4 For an excellent account of Sasanian stucco, see Kröger 1982. For examples of stucco in an early Islamic bathhouse, see Hamilton 1953.

Sasanian Silver Vessels: The Formation and Study of Early Museum Collections

by Prudence O. Harper
METROPOLITAN MUSEUM OF ART, NEW YORK

As recently as the 1950s, Sasanian and so-called Sasanian silver vessels were relatively rare works of art, represented primarily in the collection of the State Hermitage Museum and by select pieces in a few other Near Eastern, European, English and American museums. Most of the vessels had been recovered during the course of the nineteenth and early twentieth centuries in a political and cultural environment that also fostered the development of the earliest public museums. The Sasanian works came to light in the course of activities by the British in Afghanistan and India and by Russians in the mineral-rich Ural Mountain region and the Caucasus. Eventually the pieces entered museums, passing through various hands: dealers in India, British officers, agents and antiquaries, and Russian merchants and nobles.

Detailed publications of museum collections of Sasanian silver vessels began with M. Chabouillet's catalogue of the pieces in the Cabinet des Médailles et Antiques of the Bibliothèque Impériale (Chabouillet 1858). This volume was followed by the first edition of O.M. Dalton's *The Treasure of the Oxus* which appeared in 1905 (reprinted 1926 and 1964) and included not only that 'treasure' but also a number of other 'examples of early oriental metalwork' including four silver vessels described as Sasanian and post-Sasanian. All of the pieces in Dalton's publication had been bequeathed to the British Museum in 1897 by the antiquary, collector and museum keeper, Sir Augustus Wollaston Franks (1826–97) (Dalton 1964; Curtis, J.E., 1997a). In 1909 the great atlas of eastern silver and gold vessels by Yakov Ivanovich Smirnov, *Vostochnoe Serebro*, published by the Imperial Archaeological Commission, appeared. It included the silver vessels in France and England, described above, as well as other Sasanian and Sasanian-type vessels found mainly within the limits of the Russian empire and, at that time, in the Imperial Hermitage Museum and in private Russian collections (Smirnov

1909). Also in Smirnov's monumental study, of which only the plates but not the detailed text was published, was one of four Sasanian vessels that entered an American museum before 1950 (see no. 21 below).

In the earliest publications of Sasanian silver vessels classification and chronology were serious concerns. Dating Sasanian silver vessels having royal images by comparing the crowns represented with Sasanian coin images was an established method from the start and remains a valid approach. However, the difficulties inherent in establishing a chronology based solely on this feature were evident and were the focus of articles in the 1930s by Herzfeld and Erdmann who recognised that the crowns depicted on Sasanian rock reliefs and silver did not always correspond to the official coinage (Erdmann 1936, 1943; Herzfeld 1938).

As time passed, scholars gave definition to eastern schools of silver-working on the basis of archaeological and inscriptional evidence: Khoresmian, Graeco-Bactrian, and Sogdian. The term 'Sasanian', when applied to silver vessels, was used with increasing caution. Between 1935 when I.A. Orbeli published with K.V. Trever the catalogue of Sasanian silver vessels in the State Hermitage Museum, *Sasanidskii Metall*, and 1952 when Mme Trever grappled with the problem of nomenclature in an article in *Sovietskaya Arkheologiya* on so-called Sasanian objects found in the Near East and Russia, the broadly inclusive use of the term 'Sasanian' was replaced by an extremely narrow definition. Mme Trever's final position was that Sasanian works were 'those objects which were created by Persians and found in the territory of Iran (i.e. in present Persia) or beyond its borders, if they conform in iconography, style and technique with objects known as Persian-Sasanian', namely the official rock reliefs, coins and seals of officials (Trever 1952; Fajans 1957: 74–5).

While this definition of Sasanian cultural remains is, in theory, reasonable, there are certain problems in its application to the silver vessels that have survived. In the decades following Kamilla Trever's study, the corpus of silver vessels has greatly expanded, and it is evident now that by the end of the Sasanian period silver vessels in Iran were commissioned by a broad segment of a diverse population. To use the term 'Sasanian' in too narrow a context and to suggest a uniform and standardised Sasanian silver production that did not exist even at dynastic and official levels after the earliest period can be misleading.

Efforts to establish a chronology and classification of Sasanian and Sasanian-type silver vessels are seriously hindered by the absence of meaningful archaeological documentation. It is regrettably still true that the list of silver pieces found in controlled archaeological explorations in lands in the Near East where Sasanian workshops were located or, alternatively, from a provincial provenance but having a Middle Persian inscription or specific iconographical features that serve to identify them as Sasanian works of art is, even to the present day, a short one. Briefly summarised, the information is as follows:

Susa, Iran
(a) Elliptical bowl, Sb.6728; and (b) high-footed bowl, Sb.6794.
Attributed to the excavations of J. de Morgan by Pierre Amiet, who first recognised the

pieces as examples of Sasanian silverwork when he had the copper corrosion removed at the Louvre Museum in 1967. J. de Morgan began excavations at Susa in 1897.
(Amiet 1967: 277–8, figs 8–9.)

Qasr-i Abu Nasr, Iran
Hemispherical bowl, 34.107.74.
Found in the fortress area (the Sasanian citadel) during the excavations of the Metropolitan Museum of Art in 1933–4.
(Whitcomb 1985: 161, fig. 62t.)

Tal-i Malyan, Iran
Undecorated elliptical bowl.
Found in an unlined burial pit of an adult male beside the right, flexed arm with a coin of Khusro I (AD 536) or II (AD 591–628) during the excavations of the University of Pennsylvania in 1976.
(Balcer 1978: 90–2, fig. 9.)

Armazis-Khevi, Georgia
Plate with the image of a male bust enclosed within a medallion. Middle Persian inscription giving the name and lineage of Papak, the *bitiaxs*.
Found during excavations of 1937–8 in the grave of a woman and child with coins of Valerian (post AD 253), Philip the Younger (AD 247–9) and Septimius Severus (AD 201).
(Apakidze *et al.* 1958: 46–53, fig. 21, pls 47–9; Harper and Meyers 1981: 24–5, pl. 1).

Sargveshi, Georgia
Two-handled silver cup decorated with medallion images of Bahram II (AD 276–93) and members of his family. Found during excavations in 1925 on a mound and said to have come from a grave.
(Harper and Meyers 1981: 25, pl. 2.)

Less reliable than archaeological data, but a richer source of information, are comprehensive archival records of the discoveries of Sasanian silver vessels in Russia in the period roughly between 1870 and 1910. The files of various archaeological commissions are a rich source for pieces in the Hermitage Museum and were collected and studied by Kamilla Trever over the years and investigated by V.Iu. Leshchenko in his 1971 dissertation (Leshchenko 1971). Much of this information was published in 1987 in the volume by Trever and Lukonin, *Sasanidskoe Serebro*, and provides an intriguing picture of chance discoveries chiefly west of the Ural Mountains and, more occasionally, in eastern Europe in the course of farming and urban construction. Some of these Sasanian vessels have Sogdian inscriptions on them, evidence that the pieces reached lands north and west of Iran indirectly from western Central Asia. Other vessels moved north from the Near East along the rivers that connected the steppe and mountain regions with the Sasanian world. The maps in Smirnov's atlas of 1909 locate the sites of discoveries along major rivers and their tributaries: the Volga and Kama, the Don, Dnepr and Dnestr. Many Sasanian vessels found in the Ural Mountain region were recovered with Sogdian, Khoresmian and Byzantine vessels, similar objects of value. Crude drawings on some of these vessels indicate that they were secondarily used in local shamanistic cults (Leshchenko 1976).

Russia is the source too of some of the earliest Sasanian silver vessels that entered western museums. For these pieces and for others found and acquired in Iran and elsewhere the archival information is not as detailed or as accessible as the records of Russian archaeological commissions but a preliminary review of the documentation illustrates the role of historical events and of individuals in the formation of museum collections of Sasanian vessels in the nineteenth and early twentieth centuries.

Paris – Cabinet des Médailles, Bibliothèque Nationale

1 Gold, glass and rock crystal plate, Middle Persian inscription, sixth-seventh century AD, Sasanian (?). Before the French Revolution, the plate, referred to as the Cup of Solomon, was kept in the Treasury of Saint-Denis. In the early eighteenth century the vessel was identified as a Sasanian work of art. The plate was transferred to the Cabinet des Médailles in 1791. In the *Chroniques de Saint-Denis* (the most recent redaction is dated to the thirteenth century) it is claimed that Charles the Bold in AD 887 gave the plate to the Abbey of Saint-Denis. The vessel is mentioned in the legends surrounding Charlemagne (Holy Roman Emperor AD 800–14) and is described in the *Inventaires* of Saint-Denis as a gift placed at the emperor's feet by the ambassadors of the Abbasid caliph, Harun al-Rashid (r. AD 786–809). Babelon believed it to be possible that the plate came to France during the Crusades following the sack of Constantinople in AD 1204, a hypothesis given some support by a reference in an early Islamic source (Shalem 1994: 77).
(Chabouillet 1858: 364–7, no. 2538; Babelon 1900: 163–7, no. 379.)

2 Plate with a scene of a king hunting animals (Pl. 17), seventh century AD, Sasanian; gift of the duc de Luynes in 1843; noted by Smirnov (1909) as being known before 1830 and as coming from the treasure of the 'Emirs of Badakhshan'. On the interior surface of the plate between the king's head and the horse's head are traces of seven modern stamps. Two of them bear the date 1830 and one of these, rectangular in form, has a Cyrillic inscription and is probably a Russian assay mark. The other, circular, mark is unusual but also probably a state mark. Another stamp is in the shape of a shield and is, presumably, a family or individual collector mark. The three stamped numbers may be serial marks of a collection. Finally there are traces of two corners of another stamp. The fact that all the stamps appear on the face of the vessel would seem to indicate that the Sasanian plate was considered and recorded as precious metal rather than as a valued work of art.[1]

(Chabouillet 1858: 468–9, no. 2881; Smirnov 1909: pl. 31, no. 59; Aghion and Avisseau-Broustet 1994: 12–20.)

3 Plate with ceremonial scenes (Pl. 18), seventh century AD, Sasanian; acquired by Chabouillet on the Paris market in 1843 with a Sogdian silver plate decorated with a striding wolf (Chabouillet 1858: no. 2882); both vessels are noted in Smirnov (1909) to be of unknown provenance, Russia, and in the possession of the 'millionaire Russian Prince' Peter D. Soltikov (Reitlinger 1963: 89–123). In Smirnov's papers it is indicated that the plate was bought in 1843 from Soltikov and brought from Russia by M. Juste, a French restorer who worked occasionally on the arms and armour collection at Tsarskoe Selo.[2]
(Chabouillet 1858: 467, no. 3883; Smirnov 1909: pl. 57, no. 91.)

4 Ewer decorated with a design of crossed lions (Pl. 19), sixth or seventh century AD, Sasanian; acquired on the Paris market by Chabouillet for the Cabinet des Médailles in 1846; noted in Smirnov (1909) as of unknown provenance, Russia, and in the P.D. Soltikov collection. In Smirnov's papers there is a statement that the vessel was taken from Russia by M. Juste (see no. 3 above).
(Chabouillet 1858: 467, no. 2880; Smirnov 1909: pl. 51, no. 85.)

Berlin – Museum für Islamische Kunst, Staatliche Museen zu Berlin

5 Plate with a king hunting animals, seventh century AD, Sasanian or post-Sasanian, I. 4925; acquired in Paris 1926/7; noted in Smirnov (1909) as known in 1907, from Novo-Bayazet (Erevan region), Armenia and in the collection of M.P. Botkin, St Petersburg. Botkin, from a family of tea merchants, was a well-known painter, member of the Academy of Arts and collector.
(Smirnov 1909: pl. 123, no. 309; *Collection M.P. Botkine* (St Petersburg 1911), pl. 26; *Museum für Islamische Kunst: Katalog 1971*: 39, no. 100, fig. 3.)

6 Plate decorated with a griffin, seventh century AD, possibly Sasanian or post-Sasanian, I. 5384; acquired in Paris 1926/7; noted in Smirnov (1909) as known in 1907, from Novo-Bayazet (Erevan region), Armenia and in the collection of M.P. Botkin, St Petersburg. According to records in Berlin, the plate was presented to the Imperial Archaeological Commission in St Petersburg for acquisition but was refused because it was too expensive.[3]
(*Collection M.P. Botkine*, pl. 26; *Museum für Islamische Kunst: Katalog 1971*: 37, no. 90.)

7 Vase decorated with herons and trees (Pl. 20), sixth to seventh century AD, Sasanian, I. 4968; acquired in Paris 1926/7; noted in Smirnov (1909) as known before 1868, of unknown provenance, Russia, acquired at the Nizhegorodskoi fair;[4] in the collection of M.P. Botkin, St Petersburg.
(Smirnov 1909: pl. 55, no. 89; *Collection M.P. Botkine*, pl. 27; *Museum für Islamische Kunst: Katalog 1971*: 38, no. 94.)

London – The British Museum

8 Vase decorated with vintaging scenes (Pl. 21), fifth to sixth century AD, Sasanian, WAA 124094; acquired through the Franks Bequest 1897; in Dalton (1964:65) said to have been found in 1893 in a copper vase in Mazanderan, northern Iran, with no. 9 below.
(Dalton 1964: no. 209, pl. 39; Smirnov 1909: pl. 52, no. 86.)

9 Plate decorated with a banqueting scene (Pl. 22), inscribed with a Middle Persian inscription, seventh century AD, post- Sasanian (?), OA 1963–12–10,3; acquired through the Franks Bequest 1897; in Dalton (1964: 67) said to have been found with the previous vessel in 1893 in a copper vase in Mazanderan, northern Iran.
(Dalton 1964: no. 211, pl. 39; Smirnov 1909: pl. 37, no. 66.)

10 Plate illustrating an investiture scene, third-fourth century AD, Kushano-Sasanian(?), WAA 124093; acquired through the Franks Bequest 1897; in Dalton (1964: 63) said to have been obtained in Rawalpindi, India. Franks was occasionally sent material from Rawalpindi directly by dealers there (Curtis, J.E., 1997a: 242).
(Dalton 1964: no. 208, pl. 38; Smirnov 1909: pl. 16, no. 39.)

11 Plate decorated with a *senmurv* (Col. Pl. IX), seventh century AD, post-Sasanian (?), WAA 124095; in Dalton (1964: 66) reported as being acquired by the National Art Collections Fund in 1922 and presented to the British Museum. Dalton (1964: 66) states that it was 'obtained in Northern India'.
(Dalton 1964: no. 210, pl. 40.)

12 Plate decorated with a scene of a king hunting lions (Jacket; Pl. 23), sixth to seventh century AD, provincial Sasanian, WAA 124092; in Dalton (1964: 61) reported as being acquired through the Franks Bequest in 1897 and formerly in the collection of General Sir Alexander Cunningham. Major-General Sir Alexander Cunningham (1814–93) was in the Indian Army and later (1870–85) Director-General of the Archaeological Survey of India. Noted in Smirnov (1909) as 'from India to the British Museum'.
(Dalton 1964: no. 207, pl. 37; Smirnov 1909: pl. 26, no. 54.)

13 Deep plate with a scene of a king hunting stags (Col. Pl. X), fourth century AD, Sasanian, WAA 124091; according to Dalton acquired in 1908 and found in Anatolia.
(Dalton 1909; 1964: no. 206, pl. 36.)

Tehran – Muzeh Melli

14 Vase pierced at the base and decorated with dancing female figures (Pl. 24), sixth to seventh century AD, Sasanian, 2500; until 1937 recorded as being in the Gulistan Museum and after that date transferred to the Muzeh Melli.
(Godard 1938a; wrongly attributed in Vanden Berghe 1959: 6–7.)

15 Lobed bowl, sixth to seventh century AD, Sasanian, 2905; allegedly found in the neighbourhood of Qazvin in 1939.
(Godard 1938b: 305, fig. 205.)

16 Plate with an enthronement scene, sixth to seventh century AD, Sasanian, 2904; allegedly found in the neighbourhood of Qazvin in 1939 at the same time as no. 15 above.
(Godard 1938b: 301, fig. 204.)

17 Mirror cover, fifth to sixth century AD, Sasanian, 2504; described in 1938 as 'long in the Tehran Museum' and as discovered in the course of construction work for the road from Karaj to Chalus across the Elburz mountains.
(Godard 1938b: 302, fig. 206.)

18 Plate decorated with a royal onager-hunting scene, fifth to seventh century AD, Sasanian; allegedly found in Mazanderan.
(*Illustrated London News*, 21 August 1948: 214.)

Baltimore – Walters Art Gallery

19 Elliptical bowl with pointed ends (Pl. 25), decorated with enthronement scenes and dancing females, sixth to seventh century AD, provincial Sasanian or early Islamic, 57.625; acquired by Henry Walters (1848–1931) from the dealer, Joseph Brummer, in 1924. As part of Walters' bequest of his collections to the city of Baltimore, the bowl entered the newly-created museum in 1931. The museum was first opened to the public in 1934.[5]
(Harper and Meyers 1981: 119–20, pl. 36.)

20 Plate decorated with a seated king and queen (Pl. 26), sixth to seventh century AD, provincial Sasanian, 57.709; acquired by H. Walters sometime before his death in 1931 and bequeathed with no. 19 above to the city of Baltimore.
(Pope 1938: pl. 230A.)

New York – The Metropolitan Museum of Art

21 Plate decorated with a scene of a king hunting rams (Pl. 27), fifth or early sixth century AD, Sasanian, 34.33; acquired in 1934 as allegedly from Qazvin from the dealer Hagop Kevorkian who had the vessel in his possession as early as 1930. The plate was exhibited at the Kaiser Friedrich Museum in Berlin in 1930 and in the International Exhibition of Persian Art in London in 1931.
(Harper and Meyers 1981: 64–6, pl. 17.)

Washington D.C. – Freer Gallery of Art

22 Plate decorated with a scene of a king hunting boars (Pl. 28), fourth century AD, Sasanian, 34.23; acquired by the Freer Gallery of Art in 1934; noted in Smirnov (1909) as found in 1872 in Wereino, Government of Perm and in the collection of Count Stroganov, St Petersburg. The plate was in the collection of the dealer, Hagop Kevorkian in 1930. On the reverse of this vessel are identical stamps in two places, beneath the rim and within the foot ring. The stamp, a profile human head and the number 84, is a Russian assay mark guaranteeing the purity of the silver. They were, in all probability, applied following the *ukase* of 1882.[6]
(Smirnov 1909: pl. 29, no. 57; Chase 1968; Gunter and Jett 1992:106–13, no. 13.)

Sasanian or Sasanian-type vessels already lost by the early twentieth century are also known and documented by drawings and photographs. A fragment of a silver-gilded male figure once inlaid into a Sasanian plate was acquired from the Paris dealer I.E. Géjou in 1909 and was purchased through a gift from Wilhelm von Bode by the Staatliche Museen zu Berlin. Herzfeld claimed to have seen the piece on the market in Dizful, near Susa, in 1905. According to museum records, the fragment was lost, presumably stolen, between December 6 and 9, 1922.[7]

A ewer found in the Perm region was acquired by the Stroganov family in 1750 according to Smirnov who published a drawing and was in the Paris collection of Baron A.S. Stroganov in 1775 (Smirnov 1909: pl. 41, no. 79). More detailed is the history of another vessel, now lost, a Sasanian or more probably Kushano-Sasanian silver plate decorated with a hunting scene (Pl. 29). Known only from drawings published by Cunningham and Burnes in the 1840s and by Smirnov (1909: pl. 34, no.62), this plate was in the collection of the 'family of the chiefs of Budukhshan who claim descent from Alexander' until their defeat and imprisonment by their neighbour, Mir Morad Beg, ruler of Kunduz (Cunningham 1841; Burnes 1842: 203–5, pl. 18; Harper and Meyers 1981: 55–7, pls. 11a–b). The vessel then passed to the minister of the ruler of Kunduz and was purchased from this official by Dr Percival Lord in 1838. Before Dr Lord's untimely death in battle in 1840, he gave the plate to his friend and associate on the mission to Kabul, Lt Col Sir Alexander Burnes of the India Company's service, resident in Kabul in 1836–8. It is Burnes' publication of Dr Lord's account that is quoted above. With Burnes' murder in 1841 the plate was lost. Fortunately, another silver plate obtained by Dr Lord from the same source, a vessel of early Sasanian date but in a Hellenising, east Iranian style, was presented by Burnes, with Lord's permission, to the Museum of India House where it was in 1842. It was transferred from India House to the British Museum in 1900 (Dalton 1964: no. 196, pl. 27).

In the nineteenth-century records there is also evidence of replicas or forgeries of Sasanian vessels, the distinction between the two being difficult to make without any knowledge of the conditions under which the vessels were manufactured. The best known of these pieces, in the State Hermitage Museum, is an imitation of the east Iranian royal lion-hunt vessel of Sasanian date formerly in the collection of General Sir Alexander Cunningham and presented to the British Museum as part of the Franks Bequest in 1897 (no. 12 above). The copy, published by Smirnov (1909: pl. 27, no. 55) as modern and allegedly made in Rawalpindi, was acquired in the nineteenth century from Feuerdent in Paris.[8] Many details on this silver plate are so naively and inaccurately copied from the original that it is hard to believe that it was made as a forgery rather than a simple replica. A second, similar, silver 'replica' of the British Museum plate was in the collection of the dealer Hagop Kevorkian in 1937 (Morey 1937: 10; Pope 1938: pl. 231B). Both inexpert 'replicas' may have been made in Rawalpindi before the original vessel left India. This city was, at the time, a source of both reproductions and forgeries (Curtis, J.E., 1997: 234). The Kevorkian vessel, incorrectly cited in *A Survey of Persian Art* as in the State Hermitage Museum, is now lost. Finally, a reference to a third copy of the same vessel, in gold, exists in Smirnov's archives. The gold plate was known to Babelon who believed that it had been made with a silver replica (apparently Babelon knew of only one silver replica) in Peshawar.[9]

Neutron activation analysis of the silver replica in the Hermitage Museum is of interest as the vessel is almost pure unalloyed silver: 99.2% silver, 0.303% copper, 0.010% gold. The low gold content suggests that the silver source was a galena ore rather than cerussite, the source used for Sasanian silver vessels. In contrast, the original plate in the British Museum has a composition characteristic of vessels of Sasanian date: 96.4% silver, 3.02% copper, 0.63% gold.[10]

Also unclear is the identification and classification of a Sasanian-type plate published as having been found near Ardebil in northwest Iran in 1915 (Delaporte 1926; Orbeli 1938: 729–30; Herzfeld 1938: 132, fig. 16). Herzfeld records that this piece was on the market by 1923, and it was in the possession of the dealer Feuerdent by 1926 when it was published as Sasanian in the article by Delaporte. The plate, which has since vanished, is assuredly not Sasanian and the iconography and style are so remote from Sasanian works that it is hard to believe that it was originally intended to pass as a Sasanian work of art. The flat-topped weapon held by the king is a type unknown on Sasanian works and appears to fall between the categories of maces/war clubs and hurling sticks.[11] The birds on the royal garment are also distinctive and seemingly demonstrate an awareness of the figural drapery patterns on the late Sasanian rock reliefs at Taq-i Bustan.

The question of whether this plate was made deliberately as a forgery or, alternatively, as a modern adaptation in an archaising, imitative Sasanian style is difficult to answer with any certainty. As late as the nineteenth and early twentieth centuries in Iran dynastic images incorporated ancient Iranian themes and motifs. Zand and Qajar stone reliefs, one of them actually at Taq-i Bustan, include subjects drawn from Achaemenid and Sasanian art (Lerner 1980). At a lower level of society, there was also considerable interest in and a familiarity with the epic heroic past, a common subject of paintings on the walls of coffee houses in Iran (Chelkowski 1989). While no corpus of Zand or Qajar silver based on

Sasanian models has been identified, vessels of the type described above, only distantly related in style and iconography to Sasanian originals, may belong to such a class of luxury goods. One Sasanian silver plate decorated with a royal hunt in the collection of The Metropolitan Museum of Art appears to have been restored in an archaising, perhaps Qajar, style.[12]

Another context in which ancient Iranian motifs persist in the decorative arts of the nineteenth and early twentieth centuries is in works produced for the Zoroastrian community. Preserved in the Durbar Room at Osborne House, a country palace of Queen Victoria and Prince Albert on the Isle of Wight, are gifts to Victoria on the occasion of her Silver Jubilee. Among the gifts from all over the globe is an impressive silver casket decorated with motifs drawn from the Achaemenid rock carvings at Naqsh-i Rustam, a present to the Queen Empress from the Parsi community of Bombay.

Forgeries, replicas and adaptations are labels that can be applied to works varying iconographically and stylistically from ancient Sasanian originals, but distinctions between these categories are not always easy to make and the date and purpose of the creations remain elusive. Fabricated in another era, in an unknown context or environment, such works are easily misunderstood and art historical developments, modern and ancient, may pass unrecognised.

Imprecise as the records cited above are in comparison to archaeological data, they provide contemporary evidence for a trail that can be cautiously followed. Regrettably, the information that exists concerning the flood of antiquities of Sasanian date that have appeared on world markets since the 1950s is much less reliable (Dimand 1959; Dürr 1967). The growing outrage at illicit excavations and the tremendous monetary values involved have naturally led to secrecy and disinformation concerning sources and circumstances of discovery. There are no records comparable to the archives of Russian archaeological commissions and to the notes and journals of Russian landowners and merchants, of British officers, diplomats and collectors whose activities, travels and adventures led to the presence of Sasanian silver vessels in some of the earliest museum collections.

Notes

1. I am grateful to Irène Aghion, Cabinet des Médailles, Bibliothèque Nationale, for spending time with me checking the sources of the plates in the Bibliothèque Nationale and for permitting Jessie McNab, Associate Curator, European Sculpture and Decorative Arts, Metropolitan Museum, to look at the stamps. I thank Jessie McNab for her preliminary opinion on these marks.
2. Information from Smirnov's unpublished papers and on Botkin and Soltikov was provided by the late Evgeny Zeymal of the Oriental Department, State Hermitage Museum, who generously spent time investigating the records for me.
3. Jens Kröger kindly supplied additional information from the files in the Museum für Islamische Kunst in Berlin.
4. Fairs, particularly in Russia in the nineteenth and early twentieth centuries, were important sites of commercial activity. Lt. John Wood of the Indian Navy discusses this phenomenon in Burnes 1842: 347–53.
5. Information on both of the Walters Art Gallery vessels comes from the archives, courtesy of Shreve Simpson.
6. I thank Jessie McNab for this opinion.

7 Information provided by Jens Kröger.
8 Information is from the Smirnov archives, courtesy of Evgeny Zeymal.
9 Information provided by Evgeny Zeymal.
10 Neutron activation analysis and evaluation were made by Pieter Meyers, Head of Conservation, Los Angeles County Museum of Art.
11 I thank Donald J. LaRocca, Associate Curator, Arms and Armour Department, Metropolitan Museum, for advice on the weapon type.
12 Metropolitan Museum no. 57.51.19, bequest of Cora Timken Burnett, 1957. I thank Peter Chelkowski for discussing this piece and the subject of Qajar art with me. Publication of this plate with other early 'replicas' described here and elsewhere (Collon 1995: 225, fig. 193) is planned.

Mesopotamia in the Sasanian Period: Settlement Patterns, Arts and Crafts

by St John Simpson
BRITISH MUSEUM

Background

The Sasanian Empire stretched over 2000 kilometres at its greatest extent from the rolling grassy plains of northern Mesopotamia through the mountain plateau of Iran to the Central Asian steppe. The political longevity and military might of the Sasanian Empire relied on a highly efficient bureaucracy.[1] Although sadly few of the original documents survive, coins, inscribed seals and seal-impressed clay bullae that were originally attached to official documents provide means by which the Sasanian administration can be partially reconstructed (Gyselen 1989). Classical authors' accounts document Roman/Persian relations (Dodgeon and Lieu 1991), Syriac and Jewish sources provide details on indigenous religious minorities, particularly within Mesopotamia (Fiey 1965; Oppenheimer 1983) and later Arab writers describing the course of the Islamic Conquest throw further light on the human geography of Mesopotamia and Iran during the seventh century (Morony 1984).

The physical setting

The Sasanian frontiers were maintained by a standing army paid by the state but expanded at times of war through conscription. In places frontier security was ensured through the construction of elaborate 'long wall' defences; elsewhere use was made of long-distance patrols and garrison outposts. According to the Byzantine writer Procopius, the upper Khabur basin was left as a no-man's-land occupied only by seasonal bedouin between the Roman and Sasanian military lines. Mounted patrols and spies ensured that cross-border traffic was restricted to a single agreed route leading directly from Byzantine Dara to the Sasanian city and military base at Nisibis; Nisibis had been surrendered to the Sasanians after a disastrous attempt by the Roman emperor Julian to capture Ctesiphon in AD 363. The vulnerable alluvial heartland of Mesopotamia was defended by a combination of long walls, forts, long-range patrols, client Arab tribes and use of the river Euphrates as a natural barrier.

The population of Mesopotamia was highly heterogeneous. A substantial number of Persian families were transferred to Nisibis from the highland Iranian cities of Istakhr and Isfahan in order to stiffen frontier allegiances. A large Persian population also existed in Erbil, which was the seat of a major fire temple and the Persian administration of the province of Nodh-Ardashirakan (Pl. 30). From the fourth century onwards, there was also an important Christian population in this region and several of the churches in the centre of Mosul are said to have been founded in the sixth or seventh century, their floors lying up to 10 metres below present ground level owing to the gradual rise in the level of the surrounding properties (Fiey 1959). Christianity also flourished along the desert margin and in the Persian Gulf where a large number of monasteries and churches were founded as late as the eighth or ninth century. Late Sasanian and Early Islamic churches have now been excavated at a number of sites in this region, including Ain Shai'a, al-Qusair North and al-Hira in the Iraqi Western Desert and on the Gulf islands of Akkaz, Failaka, Kharg and Sir Bani Yas (Okada 1992; King 1997).

The lowland alluvial plains of southern Mesopotamia and southwest Iran reached their economic peak during the Sasanian period (Fig. 12). Heavy Sasanian state investment in the economic infrastructure boosted the Mesopotamian economy, stimulated further by the maintenance of the capital at Ctesiphon, on the river Tigris some 35 kilometres south of Baghdad. Massive new irrigation projects were constructed, resulting in trunk canals linking the Euphrates and Tigris, and the massive Nahrawan/Katul-i Kisrawi canal system that was fed by water drawn from the Lesser Zab, Adheim, Tigris and Diyala rivers (Adams 1965, 1981; Gibson 1972; Wenke 1975–6). Surveys also demonstrate intensive irrigation networks across the alluvial plains on a scale never previously attempted. The purpose of these waterworks was to increase and regularise the flow of water so as to ensure double-cropping and improved agricultural yields. Greater taxes ensured a greater flow of money into the treasury, facilitating further investment in capital projects and maintenance of the army (Howard-Johnston 1995). Settlements sprawled alongside the new canals, leading to a pattern of ribbon development, and rural settlement programmes were enforced with transfer of populations to new 'virgin land' schemes. Few of these rural sites have yet been excavated although a sequence of Sasanian and Early Islamic pottery was retrieved from a small village site called Tell Abu Sarifa, near Nippur (Adams 1970).

Cities were founded at strategic river crossings, such as Nineveh on the Tigris or Naw Gird (Arab Haditha, presently the site of Kushaf) at the junction of the Greater Zab and Tigris. Nestorian bishops are attested from Nineveh for AD 554, 576 and 585 and the emperor Heraclius crossed the Tigris at this point prior to the battle of Nineveh in 628. Excavations conducted here on behalf of the British Museum by Layard, Loftus, Rassam, King and Campbell Thompson produced an important corpus of Sasanian material from this site, including several coin-hoards, incantation bowls, seals, bullae, helmets, other metalwork, pottery and glassware (Simpson 1996).

Other old urban centres in southern Mesopotamia, including Babylon, Borsippa, Nippur and Uruk, continued as important market towns. Many of these are referred to in Arab Conquest accounts and each has produced large amounts of Sasanian pottery and other datable material. One characteristic class of Late Sasanian object that was particularly widely used at these traditional urban centres are the so-called 'incantation bowls' (Pl. 31). These are ordinary domestic bowls and lids that were used to record spells recited by local

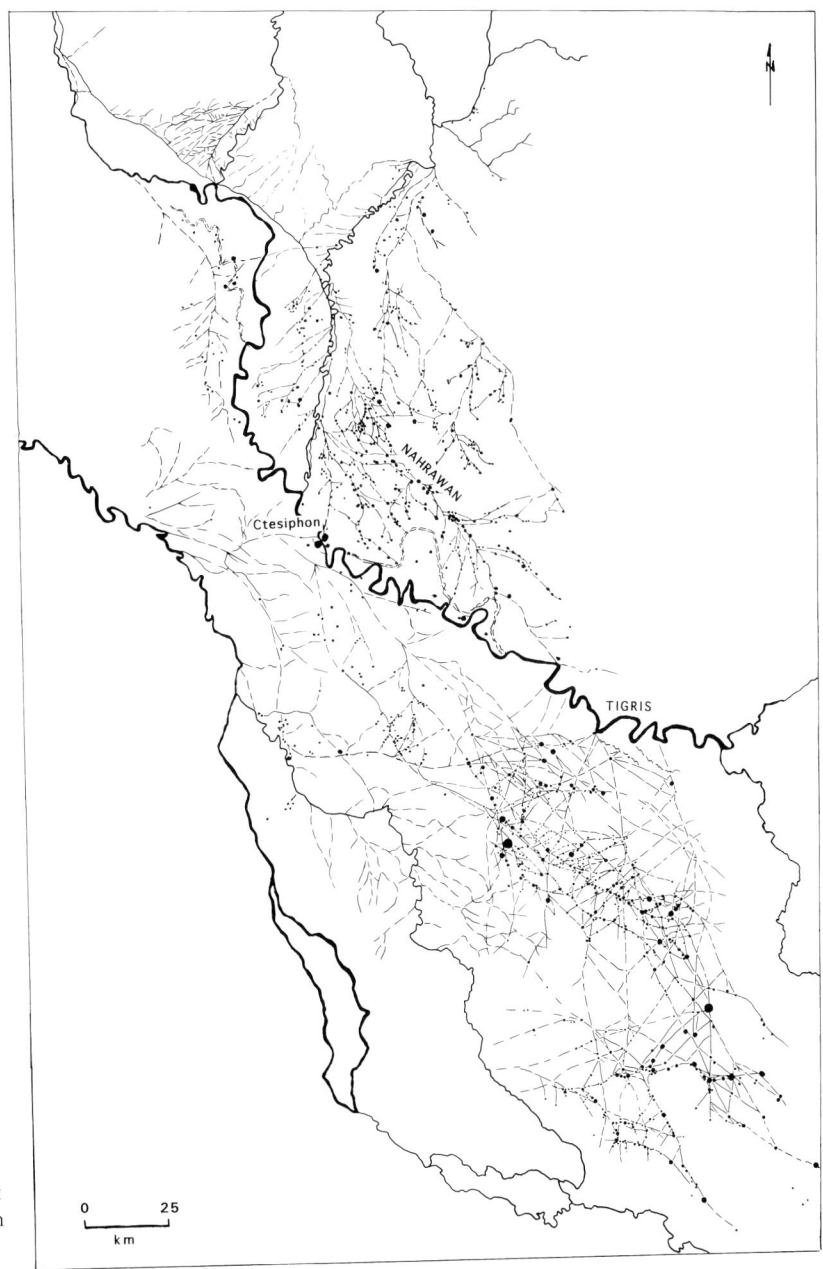

12 Map showing Sasanian settlement patterns in southern Mesopotamia.

exorcists attempting to drive out demons lurking within the household or cemetery. The spells were usually written in Aramaic but Mandaic, Syriac, Middle Persian and gobbledegook versions are also represented in the extensive British Museum collection. The texts underline the mixed population and the agricultural setting of the region: cattle, sheep, goats and chickens are frequently listed among the possessions of the house-owner (Yamauchi 1967; Naveh and Shaked 1993).

A more important contemporary source for reconstructing the Mesopotamian economy during this period is the Babylonian Talmud, compiled between the third and fifth centuries for legal reference by the substantial local Jewish community (Newman 1932; Oppenheimer 1983). Fallowing, crop rotation, multiple cropping, manuring and cross ploughing were standard agricultural practices with cultivation of wheat, barley, dates and a range of other crops. The density of cultivation occasioned one Syriac author to comment

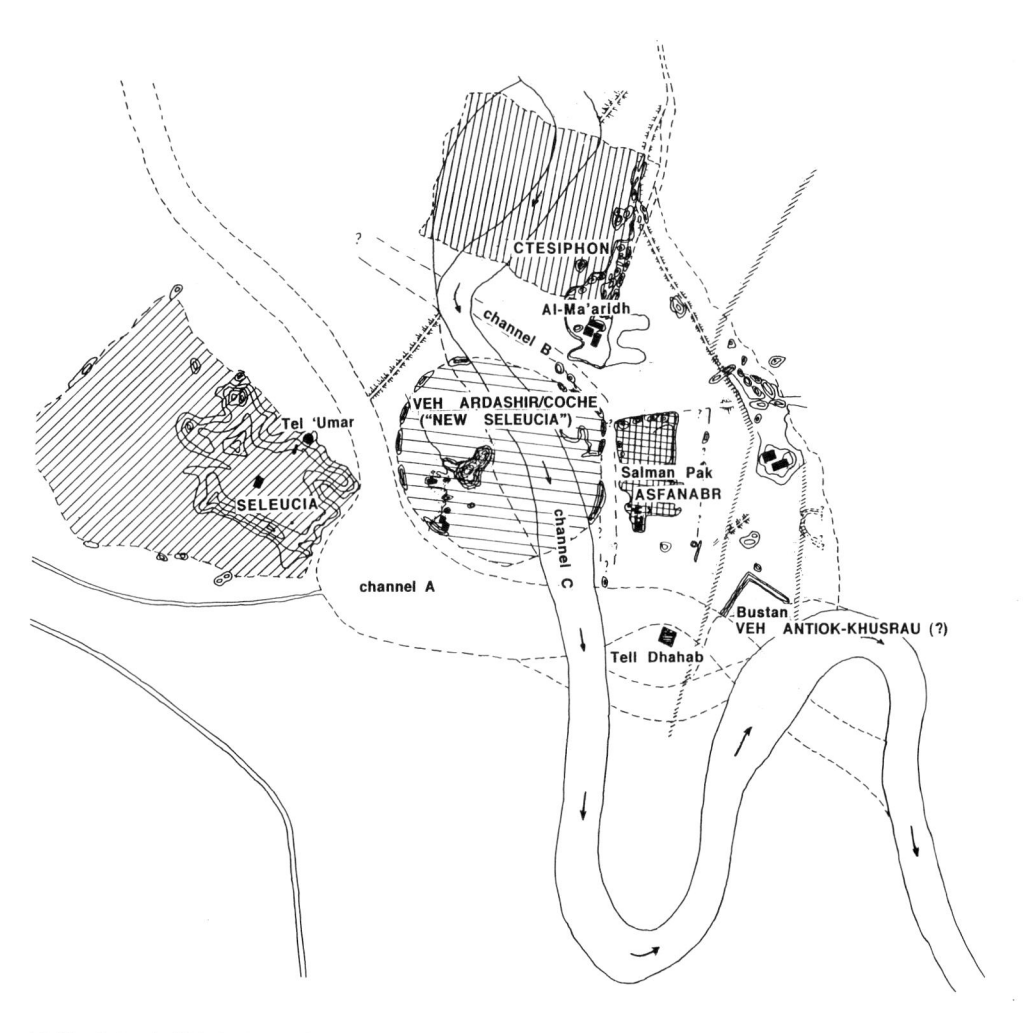

13 The Seleucia-Veh Ardashir-Ctesiphon conurbation.

that a squirrel need never touch the ground between Ctesiphon and the Gulf (Wigram 1929: 48).

The intensive agriculture was capable of supporting a high population density and several new cities were also found. One of these was Veh Ardashir ('The city of Ardashir') that was founded by Ardashir I (*c.* AD 224–40) on the site of a village called Kokhé (often spelt as Choche), on the right bank of the river Tigris. This was deliberately sited next to the old Hellenistic city of Seleucia on the Tigris, and opposite the Partho-Sasanian capital of Ctesiphon (Fig. 13), to which Veh Ardashir was linked by a pair of bridges; the close physical relationship led to the two cities being twinned as 'the cities' (Arabic *al-Mada'in*). The reason for Ardashir's new foundation was probably partly political but also appears to have been pragmatic as excavations within Seleucia suggest that by the third century AD it had become over-congested. The old city-site of Seleucia was soon deserted apart from the construction of a massive lookout tower at Tell Umar, and use of the ruins as a place of execution and burial (Simpson 1997a).

Veh Ardashir, also referred to as 'New Seleucia', was designed as a circular city with horseshoe-shaped interval towers, 10 metre thick fortifications, and rectangular blocks of housing separated by broad asphalted roads and smaller streets or alleys. Two complete blocks were excavated by an Italian expedition (Fig. 14). The courtyard house-plans were built in a local Mesopotamian mudbrick tradition but included Persian barrel-vaulted reception *ivans* facing onto the courtyard. The discovery of iron and glass slag, and a number of plaster moulds for casting furniture fittings, suggests the presence of small craft workshops interspersed with residential houses.[2] Contemporary historical sources indicate that there was a major citadel, prison, fire-temple and a rabbinical academy in Veh Ardashir; a long barrel-vaulted Christian church has been excavated at the site.

Across the river, Ctesiphon also appears to have been strongly fortified with fired brick walls and a moat, and bisected by a canal that fed into the Tigris. According to an early seventh century source compiled for the Chinese court (*Chou-shu*), its population numbered 'more than 100,000 households' (Miller 1959: 13). However, despite its significance as the Partho-Sasanian imperial capital, Ctesiphon has never been archaeologically explored apart from brief German excavations of a series of very large mudbrick villas or palaces near the edge at a spot called al-Ma'aridh. The walls of these buildings were decorated with carved stuccoes, a characteristic feature of the period (Kröger 1982). There were several other towns and cities in the vicinity, including the site of el-Bustan which may be identified with the city called Veh Antioch Khusro (Khusro's City of Antioch), that was settled with deportees from Khusro I's second sack of Antioch in AD 542.

Approximately 2 kilometres south of Ctesiphon, on the opposite bank to Veh Ardashir, lay the Late Sasanian royal city of Aspanabr. This appears to have been founded in response to congestion within Ctesiphon itself and the growing needs of the imperial administration. It contained the royal stables, parks, an aviary and several large palaces, including that of the archbishop. Many of the buildings here have been badly damaged by later brick robbing or remain covered beneath an Early Islamic settlement at Salman Pak,

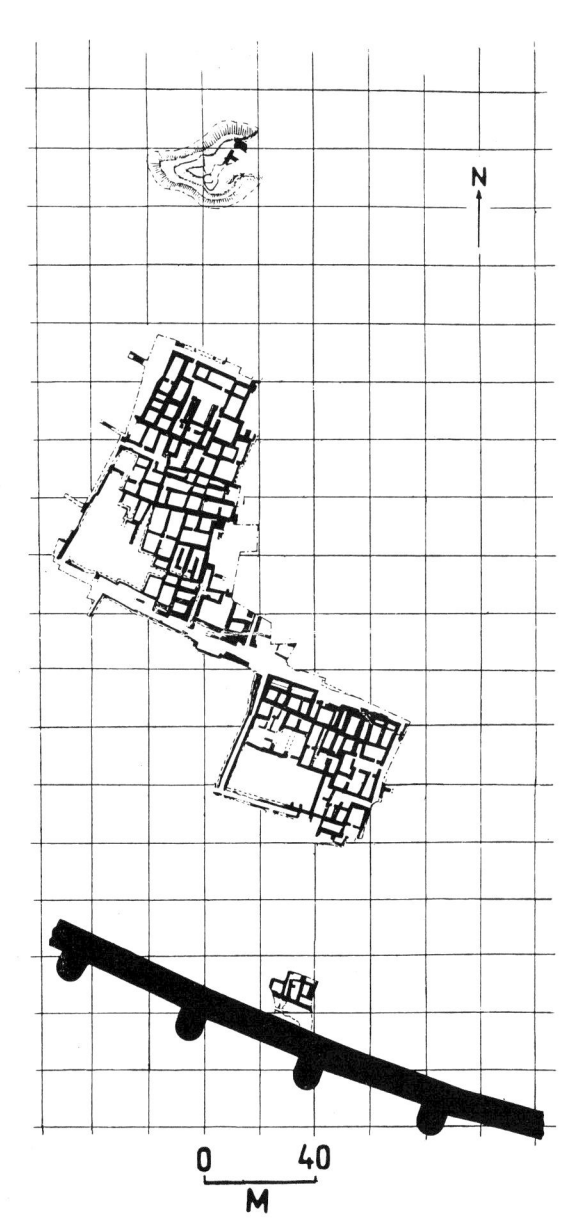

14 Plan of excavated Sasanian architecture and the nearby fortifications in the southern quarter of Veh Ardashir.

yet the single surviving monument is one of the outstanding architectural achievements of Sasanian architects. Popularly known as the Taq-i Kisra (Throne of Khosro), it consists of a massive barrel-vaulted *ivan*, with a bath-house and other buildings concealed behind a huge façade that faced onto a large open courtyard (Pl. 32). This *ivan* functioned as a grander equivalent of the type of reception room found in large courtyard houses in Veh Ardashir. This complex may have been the very same palace of Khosro that, according to the Byzantine author Procopius, was decorated with 'Greek' marble and constructed with the help of 'craftsmen skilled in ceilings' sent by Justinian; fragments of imported marble, glass tesserae and carved stuccoes were discovered nearby during excavations (Kröger 1982).

The location of Ctesiphon as the imperial capital within the heart of Mesopotamia underlines the economic and cultural importance of this region, which must have been stimulated further by the presence and patronage of the Court.

Arts and crafts

The Sasanian Empire – often referred to simply as 'Persia' – enjoyed a reputation for luxury in Byzantine and Arab written accounts. A seventh-century Chinese account of the 'Western Nations' included a lengthy section on 'Po-ssu' (Persia). Its king 'sits on a golden sheep couch,[3] and wears on his head a gold-flowered cap. He is clad in a brocade robe and a woven skirt, both decorated with pearls and precious objects.' The author goes on to describe the country and its customs, closing with a long list of Sasanian products:

'white ivory, lions, ostrich eggs, genuine pearls, mock pearls, glass, coral, amber, ceramic glazes, agate, crystal, emerald [?], gold, silver, zinc ore, diamonds, red beads, steel, iron, bronze, tin, vermilion, mercury, damask brocade, white cotton cloth, felt, woollen rugs, red roebuck hide, as well as frankincense [?], saffron, storax, 'dark wood' and other aromatics, black pepper, pippal [pepper], crystallised honey, date palms, monkshoods and wolfbanes, myrobalan, oak galls, 'salty green', orpiment and other products' (Miller 1959).

The list appears to focus on high-value low-bulk commodities considered desirable in the Chinese court, many of which recur in later Tang dynasty records of Western imports, yet it also provides a vivid impression of Sasanian arts and crafts that is supported by archaeological finds and other historical references.

Various other luxury materials are attested from the archaeological record. Ostrich eggs, imported from Arabia and modified for use as containers, have been excavated at Aspanabr and Qasr-i Abu Nasr (Whitcomb 1985: 196–7, fig. 74i). A late Sasanian ivory chessman in the form of a kneeling warrior was excavated at Ctesiphon, closely paralleling pieces found at Qasr-i Abu Nasr in Fars and the Afrasiab area (Whitcomb 1985: 190, 194–5, fig. 73a). These archaeological finds support literary evidence which suggests the transmission of the game from India to Iran in the sixth century. Seed-pearls, presumably from Persian Gulf or Indian fisheries, were sewn onto clothing, belts and headdresses, and larger examples were attached to earrings; pearls were discovered in Sasanian graves at Tell Mohammed Arab, a passage in the Talmud refers to 'a valuable slave who was expert in perforating pearls' (Newman 1932: 70) and 'two chests containing pearls' were seized by Arab forces after the battle of Nahavand in AD 641 (Hitti 1916: I, 474–5). Coral was probably imported from the Red Sea and amber is presumed to be a Baltic import via the Russian 'fur route': both materials have been found in the form of beads in Sasanian graves in Mesopotamia.

Agate, carnelian, rock crystal, opal, amethyst and lapis lazuli are likewise attested from 'late graves' in Mesopotamia, including Tell Mohammed Arab near Eski Mosul. This site also produced evidence for Late Sasanian etched carnelian beads, derived from a much older Indian bead tradition. Tabular or rough spherical carnelian beads were crudely etched with a natural alkali to create patterns in white on a pinkish or reddish stone; some of the designs include Sasanian 'devices' and crosses (Roaf 1984: 143–4, pl. XIc). This particular type of etched carnelian bead is also found in Iran and Central Asia but is absent from South Asia, suggesting that it was produced within the Sasanian Empire itself. Hardstones such as agate and carnelian were also preferred materials for making Sasanian stamp seals (Col. Pl. XI; Bivar 1969). Replication experiments and scanning-electron-microscopy of the perforations suggest that some 5% of Sasanian seals in the Metropolitan Museum of Art were perforated using diamond drill-bits, explaining a Tang Dynasty reference to the Persian export of diamond drill-bits to China (Gorelick and Gwinnett 1990; Laufer 1919: 521).

Literary allusions to Sasanian uses of steel, notably for sword blades, have been recently confirmed by new technical analyses in the British Museum that provide evidence for crucible-steel, in this case to make double-edged sword blades fitted with elaborate silver or gold hilts and scabbards that were decorated with an all-over feather or scale pattern; these swords date to the seventh century and derive from northern Iran (Pl. 33; Craddock, Lang and Simpson in press; Overlaet 1982). Early Islamic descriptions and the discovery of a ninth/tenth century crucible-steel workshop at the city of Merv suggest continuity of this Sasanian industry in Khurasan (Herrmann *et al.* 1997: 10–13).

A variety of cheap hemp, woollen, and finer linen and cotton textiles were produced in other regions of the Empire, notably the Mesopotamian and Susian lowlands. Flax-beaters, fullers, linen-bleachers, dyers, carpet-weavers, spinners and tailors are mentioned occasionally and the towns of Be-Mikse, Pumbadita on the middle Euphrates and Nehar-Abba are referred to as textile centres (Newman 1932: 104–5; Tafazzoli 1974; Oppenheimer 1983: 91). Sadly, few Sasanian textiles have survived apart from a small number identified from Egypt or in European treasuries but some coloured silk, cotton, wool and felt fragments have been excavated in graves at Shahr-i Qumis in north-east Iran and Tal-i Malyan in Fars (Balcer 1978; Vogelsang-Eastwood 1988). The emphasis in ancient written sources was on colour ('Indian purple', 'emerald-green', 'red women's robes', 'vermilion dyes'), coloured fringes, gold brocade and lightness but more elaborate figural designs enclosed within repeating roundels appear at the end of the period, judging by depictions at the seventh-century grotto of Taq-i Bustan. A further instance of economic continuity from the Late Sasanian to Early Islamic periods is illustrated by the discovery of carbonised cotton seeds in fifth-century and later contexts at Merv (Herrmann *et al.* 1995: 51). Cotton is a summer crop and its primary use is as a source of fibre although useful by-products include seed-cake fodder and oil. Successful cultivation requires large quantities of water, implying carefully maintained irrigation systems. Khurasan was attested as a major cotton-textile producing region during the ninth century and later but this evidence again suggests a Sasanian – if not earlier – origin for this industry (see Lamm 1937: 95–9, 199–200).

Unfortunately, little is known in detail about the actual craftsmen themselves although archaeological and historical sources add some information. According to the Avesta, they belonged to the so-called 'fourth class' of society, grouped together with peasants but lower in social status than priests, warriors and bureaucrats. Syriac sources suggest the organisation of urban crafts into guilds, each with its own 'chief of the artisans'; segregation of industry is suggested by another source as 'every trade had its own series of shops in the bazaar' (Tafazzoli 1974). The result may have been not dissimilar to a traditional Middle Eastern bazaar; indeed the Byzantine Greek word *pazari* is a loan-word from Persian (Shahbazi 1990: 594). A variety of specialised craftsmen are mentioned, including textile-workers, tent-makers, butchers, tanners, leather-workers, saddlers, shoe-makers, string- or rope-makers, carpenters, furniture-joiners and painters; goldsmiths, silversmiths, iron-smiths, cup-makers, jewellers, perfumers, potters and brick manufacturers are also attested (Cohen 1937; Tafazzoli 1974; Levy 1985). Most of these crafts were probably urban but some flourished in the countryside. A passage in the Babylonian Talmud refers to 'basket makers having brought baskets to Babylon' (Oppenheimer 1983: 46) and archaeological surface surveys indicate large-scale brick, pottery and glass production at industrial settlements located on major waterways.

Unlike many of the other – particularly perishable – crafts mentioned above, pottery and glass normally survive in quantity. Sasanian pottery was mass-produced and designed for everyday use. The markedly regionalised traditions of the Parthian period were gradually unified and there is greater evidence for the influence of metalware forms on the shapes of Sasanian ceramic pourers. This is illustrated by the sharply everted rims, moulded ribs at the shoulder-neck junctions and elegant pear-shaped vessel profiles found on these vessels. A particularly striking instance of skeuomorphism is illustrated by a small group of ceramic pitchers from the Dailaman region of northwest Iran which were decorated in imitation repoussé and coloured yellow in imitation of gilding (Simpson 1998). Within Mesopotamia the indigenous glaze tradition had a major impact on ceramics produced in the Ctesiphon area where a high proportion of the excavated vessels and even the cooking wares were covered with green or blue alkaline glazes coloured with metal oxides. In other parts of Mesopotamia and Iran, however, local styles of plainwares and coarsewares predominated. In northern Mesopotamia, these included a tradition of decorating jars with specially carved large wooden stamps (Pl. 34; Curtis, J.E., 1997b). These were repeatedly impressed into the vessel walls to create repetitive rows of animals, crosses or geometric designs enclosed within roundels or square borders (Col. Pl. XII). Popularity of the cross motif underlines the importance of the local Christian population (Simpson 1997b).

Glassware was also manufactured to satisfy local and court demand for practical and attractive containers. Mesopotamia appears to have been the centre of this industry, judging by the number of glass-producing sites reported from surface surveys and the relative quantity of glassware excavated at sites in the region compared to highland Iran or Central Asia. Small bottles were blown from coloured glass: some were left plain but others were dipped into patterned plaster moulds to create shallow ribbed decoration that was sometimes pinched (so-called 'nip't diamond wares') with iron pincers. These vessels were used to contain ointments, perfumes and make-up and often were deposited as grave-goods. Their fabrics, thick walls and decoration differ from contemporary Roman wares and suggest that Sasanian glassworkers operated independently from contemporary glasshouses in the eastern Roman Empire. These two traditions effectively combined after the Arab Conquest.[4]

Sasanian luxury glassware was even more distinctive. There is very little evidence for the application of secondary colours to glassware or the manufacture of gold-glass in the Sasanian world: instead the preferred technique was cold-working of blanks that were deliberately blown or cast from near-colourless, brownish or greenish fabrics. These vessels usually consisted of open bowls and pourers decorated with rows of cut facets. During the sixth and early seventh centuries these were overlapped to create multiple reflective and sparkling surfaces (Col. Pl. XIII). Cut glass Sasanian bowls were particularly highly prized in the East where they recur in tombs and Buddhist sites across northern China, Korea and Japan (Fukai 1977). Surprisingly, Sasanian cut glass has not been reported from the Roman world or from the Indian sub-continent, perhaps reflecting the preferred use in those regions of local Roman or Indian luxury wares.

Conclusion

Studies of Sasanian material culture have tended to focus on the fine arts rather than evidence for everyday crafts. Furthermore, these have been traditionally viewed within a strictly Iranian context. Systematic and fully published excavations of Sasanian sites are regrettably scarce, yet surface surveys, discoveries and material found particularly in early explorations or recent salvage projects throw considerable further light on the sites, settlement patterns, and arts and crafts of this period. The deliberate siting of the capital at Ctesiphon – rather than at the family seat of Istakhr or another Iranian city – and the extensive investment in urban and royal infrastructure across Mesopotamia imply a high degree of court patronage and local consumer demand. The possible significance of indigenous Mesopotamian craftsmen has almost certainly been underestimated. The strength of the Mesopotamian economy was its agriculture and its ability to sustain a dense population. There are strong elements of cultural continuity from the Parthian period, for instance in pottery production, yet similarities in form between certain Roman and Sasanian metal and glassware types suggests that there were also cross-cultural stimuli. Within this context, it is interesting to note that remarkably few objects of foreign manufacture have been discovered within the closely defined borders of the Sasanian Empire. These include a handful of Late Roman/Early Byzantine gold and bronze coins (Hobbs 1995) and in addition, a bronze lamp and fragments of blue-spotted Eastern Roman glass lamps from Nineveh and Veh Ardashir (Simpson 1996) and a Gandharan sculpture from Veh Ardashir (Invernizzi 1968–9) that may derive from specifically Christian or Buddhist religious contexts. Conversely, there is surprisingly little evidence for Sasanian material from the Roman Empire or India, although coins, beads, silver, cut glass and pottery trickled northwards into Russia (Frye 1972), eastwards through Central Asia to the Far East (Kröger 1979; Thierry 1993) or around the Arabian peninsula as far as Southern Arabia and the Horn of Africa (Sedov 1992; Smith and Wright 1988).[5] Much remains to be done in terms of archaeological investigation and scientific analysis yet the available evidence points to a rich Sasanian heritage that exerted a strong influence into the later Umayyad and Abbasid periods.

Notes

1 See Christensen (1936), Ghirshman (1962) and Herrmann (1977) for the background on the Sasanian Empire. Many of the most important pieces are illustrated by Harper *et al.* (1978) and in *Splendeur des Sassanides,* catalogue of exhibition at Musées royaux d'Art et d'Histoire, Brussels 1993.

2 Similar evidence exists from Sasanian residential areas recently excavated at the city of Merv, in the northeastern Sasanian province of Khurasan, specifically in the form of iron smithing-hearth bottoms, spindle whorls and worked horn and bone offcuts (Herrmann *et al.* 1997: 9).

3 See Curtis, V.S., 1996: 240.

4 Compositional analyses of excavated Sasanian glass from Mesopotamia are currently underway in the British Museum Department of Scientific Research with the view of characterising the local glassware fabrics.

5 Robin *et al.* (1997: 209) illustrate Sasanian coloured glassware and a fine shallow bowl decorated with cut circular facets that appear to have been found in a tomb in al-Jawf. The published description as second-third century Alexandrian is erroneous.

Sasanian Art beyond the Persian World

by Guitty Azarpay
The University of California, Berkeley

Persian art of the Sasanian period, like that of the Achaemenid and the Safavid dynasties, is generally held to have profoundly influenced the arts of Iran's neighbours and trading partners. The spread of Sasanian courtly symbols such as royal enthronements, hunts and embellished animal motifs beyond the Persian world, particularly along the Silk Road, is usually cited in support of that claim.

In this paper I propose to examine the phenomenon of the appeal of Sasanian art beyond the Persian world by exploring that art's function and its perceived meaning. My preliminary observations on the history of Sasanian art, which, unavoidably, return to monuments treated from other perspectives in earlier papers presented in this seminar, are aimed at explaining the meaning of Sasanian art by reference to its function, and to its conceptual framework which finds rich documentation in Zoroastrian sources. The fascination with Sasanian art, and its widespread imitation beyond the Persian world, are here traced not only to the courtly overtones of that art, but also to its underlying socio-religious meaning. In conclusion, the enhanced image of the material world, which pervades all aspects of Sasanian art, is explained as a reflection of the ancient Iranian notion of the material world as god's good creation and as a weapon in his cosmic struggle against evil.

1 Patterns of Meaning in Sasanian Art

I begin with a review of some general patterns of meaning conveyed in works of art that span the Sasanian age from its foundation in AD 224 through the reign of Khusro II, in the early seventh century.

A principal achievement of the Sasanian dynasty, as noted by previous speakers, is its replacement of feudal leadership with centralised authority, topped by the king. As persuasively argued by Richard Frye, Sasanian Iran, which remained a highly centralised state for over 400 years, forged a fusion of the offices of church and state, of religious authority and secular rule. As head of state, the dynasty's founder Ardashir (AD 224–241), a descendant of the Zoroastrian priesthood of Fars, also assumed guardianship of the sacred fire, the symbol of the national religion. This is explicit on Sasanian coins, where the reigning monarch with his crown and regalia of office appears on the obverse, backed by the sacred fire, the symbol of the national religion, on the coin's reverse. The merging of the functions of church and state are reflected also in the architecture and the monumental art of the Sasanian period, treated in some detail in the foregoing papers.

The search for the meaning in Sasanian art requires consideration of that art's function, of the ways art is used in Sasanian society. It is generally agreed that Sasanian monumental art, known from rock reliefs and large-scale sculpture, like Sasanian architecture, is the expression strictly of the bureaucratic elite. It is the values of this elite that also inspire Sasanian *decorative arts*, such as silver vessels, patterned textiles, and engraved gems.

These are generally portable, functional, and often high-value articles, produced for special purposes such as official donations, awards, payments in kind, and commercial exchange. Sasanian decorated silver and patterned silks are best known, in fact, from hoards and finds at sites outside Iran, where they were traded, treasured and imitated. It is remarkable that even the small category of artefacts that was produced for members of the Sasanian middle class echoes the prevailing artistic style of the elite. St John Simpson has drawn attention to some of the artefacts produced for the middle class in Sasanian times. A notable distinction of this art is perhaps its admission of popular and folkloric motifs, found on some textiles, in stucco decoration from modest buildings, and on personal sealstones, gems and amulets.

Like monumental Sasanian architecture, in which the functional and symbolic needs of the elite are met in the construction of royal palaces and religious foundations, Sasanian art proclaims the message of its patrons in its form and function. To illustrate the point, I return briefly to a monument that on a number of occasions has received careful and thorough consideration by Dr Herrmann. This is the equestrian investiture of Ardashir I by the god Ahuramazda, or Ohrmazd, at Naqsh-i Rustam (Pl. 35). Carved directly beneath the Old Persian rock-cut tombs of Achaemenid kings, Ardashir at once links the past with the present and the future in a remarkably dynamic and terse statement on his material and spiritual victory, and on the dynasty's bond with the national religion. In a powerfully balanced and symmetrical composition, the king confronts his god at the moment of their respective triumphs, in which the king's achievements in the battlefield are equated with those of the god on the spiritual front. Ardashir's defeat of the last Parthian ruler, prostrated before his horse, is echoed in the creator god's ultimate defeat of the Evil Spirit, Ahriman, shown in an equivalent position. The king's merit is rewarded by the god with the diadem, or *farr*, of divine kingship. The equation of king and god, of the real and the ideal, are here echoed in the form of a graphic refrain that lends a cosmic dimension to historical reality. The king-god equation also recalls the Zoroastrian notion that derives material creation from a spiritual prototype.

What makes the scene compelling to the viewer is its double meaning or, perhaps, its multi-valence. The scene is set in virtual space, and at an imaginary point in time, where and when the king is symbolically rewarded for a historic triumph that mirrors the god's cosmic struggle (cf. Williams and Boyd 1993). The focus here on the act of investiture combined with the reverential, sober and significant gestures of the participants endow the scene with subtle overtones of the concept of good deeds performed and rewarded.

Of special importance for the topic of the present paper is the merging of the role of Ardashir as a specific, historical ruler with his generic function as culture-hero and god's champion. The generic overtones and multiple layers of meaning observed in this composition are abundantly attested in all subsequent Sasanian reliefs that depict seemingly historical documentaries. A similar merging of real or historical events with ideal or generic notions is notable in the decorative arts of the Sasanian period. It is during the reign of Shapur II (AD 309–79) that Sasanian art finds unsurpassed expression in the applied arts, particularly in the splendid medium of decorated silver. As observed by Prudence Harper (1978), Sasanian silver plates, decorated with elegant and dazzling expressions of courtly art, were largely produced in royal workshops under Shapur II, when the image of Shapur as a *royal hunter*, is creatively rendered in numerous variations. Shapur's reign is also an age of religious awakening. When threatened by an ascendant East Roman empire in the fourth century, Shapur adopts new administrative and military strategies, and as counterpoise to the recently Christianised Roman world, he vigorously enforces Zoroastrian religious orthodoxy in Iran. The subject matter of much of the art of this period is courtly and celebratory; the ruling elite is shown in the performance of symbolic and official acts, such as the royal hunt, the banquet, or at enthronements. The king, with crown and regalia, is the principal actor in these scenes. Yet his individual identity and the specific event chronicled are invariably subordinated to his generic role as culture-hero and paragon of Zoroastrian virtues.

A most remarkable expression of the Sasanian concept of the ideal ruler is formulated in late Sasanian times, when under Khusro I (531–79), the king assumes greater royal prerogative. The distinctive crown engraved on the celebrated rock-crystal inlay from the so-called 'Cup of Solomon', in the Bibliothèque Nationale in Paris identifies its wearer as Khusro I (Pl. 36). Yet the stiff and frontal posture of the enthroned king imparts a remote and superhuman quality to the image. The universal appeal of this late Sasanian concept of quintessential kingship is attested by the preservation of the bowl as a cherished treasure in a European collection, and by its imitation beyond the Persian world. A detail from a Coptic textile, from Antinoe, Egypt, shared between the Louvre and the Textile Museum at Lyon, recalls the familiar Sasanian enthronement scene in a fabric that dates to AD 619–29, the period of the Sasanian Persian occupation of Egypt (Col. Pl. XIV) (Ghirshman 1962: fig. 244; Martiniani-Reber and Bénazeth 1997: no. 69).

Charismatic kingship in Sasanian art finds its fullest expression in the monumental reliefs of Khusro II (590–628), from the rock-cut grotto of Taq-i Bustan, near Kermanshah, dated to the early seventh century (Fig. 15; Fukai and Horiuchi 1969–84;

15 The arched facade of the larger rock-cut vault at Taq-i Bustan, near Kermanshah.

Movassat 1988). The display of symbols of majesty, echoed throughout the decorative assemblage of the large vault at this site, remains such a striking panegyric to kingship, that the grotto was chosen as the setting for a royal relief as recently as the nineteenth century.[1] The larger of two vaults cut into the Kuh-i Paru, the outcrop of rock overlooking the Sasanian park and hunting preserve, is entered through an arched facade, embellished with stylized floral scrolls topped with a pair of winged figures. Like winged victories on the Roman triumphal arch, these figures converge from the spandrels of the arch bearing symbols of kingship and bounty. The diadem of divine rule, held by these figures, and telescoped around the frame of the large vault, is extended to the solemn and frontal king by flanking gods, in the investiture scene carved against the vault's back wall (Pl. 16). Whereas in the early Sasanian investiture of Ardashir (Pl. 35), the king claims the symbolic diadem through the merit of his deeds, in Khusro's investiture, divine favour appears as a corollary of kingship, as part and parcel of the royal office. Poised below the investiture scene is the king's equestrian image as an armoured knight. Although the king's individual identity is concealed behind the chain camail of his helmet and his armour, his generic identity is displayed in every detail of his posture, gesture and dress that present him in the role of a heroic warrior, identified in Zoroastrian sources with the ideal king (Herzfeld 1920: 71; Erdmann 1937: 79).

2 The Appeal of Sasanian Art

The appeal of Sasanian art and its extraordinary renaissance along the Silk Road and in the early Muslim world was to a large extent inspired by courtly motifs of material bounty and by symbols of charismatic kingship, such as those found in the reliefs from the large vault at Taq-i Bustan (Pl. 37). Nowhere is the appeal of Sasanian art more remarkable than at the imperial court of Tang China, from the seventh to the ninth centuries (AD 618–906), which on the death of the last Sasanian king, Yazdigird III, in AD 642, gave sanctuary to the Sasanian crown prince Peroz, and to his retinue. At the start of China's cosmopolitan Tang dynasty, the high point in East-West exchange, China received some 30 missions from the Sasanian empire, and thousands of Persians resided and conducted business in the western market place of the Chinese capital at Chang-an, present-day Xsian.

Persians figure among other Westerners who fascinated the Chinese and are similarly immortalised in figurines from tombs of the Tang period. Dressed in their distinctive headgear, trousers and tailored jackets, Persians travelled the long distance across the Takla Makan desert, in Asia's heartland, on horseback. Their merchandise was carried by the hardy Bactrian camel that proudly postures among the remarkable earthenware figurines from Xsian (Col. Pl. XV). Although silk was the major export from China, other sorts of commodities changed hands in the many stations along the Silk Road.

The admiration of Sasanian art by the Chinese is attested in imported Sasanian vessels and in their Chinese imitations. Sasanian and East Iranian metalwork was collected and creatively imitated in Tang China, as attested by imported ewers, lobed cups and bowls, and rhytons, and by their local imitations. A distinctive Iranian shape is the rhyton, the horn-shaped vessel with a base in the form of an animal's head, used for drinking wine, represented by an example in the Arthur Sackler Gallery of Art in Washington DC (Pl. 38), and by its imagery on a bowl in the Cleveland Museum of Art. A variant of this vessel, carved from onyx, found in a tomb in the vicinity of Xsian, finds parallels in drinking vessels used by banqueters in Sogdian wall paintings (Gunter and Jett 1992: 205–10).

In silver-poor China, Sasanian metalwork was only occasionally reproduced in gold and silver. More numerous, however, are mould-made versions cast in baser metals, and imitations in glazed ceramics. Particularly striking are the shapes of Tang earthenware and their bold and non-Chinese relief decoration which is highlighted with splashes of metallic colours (Col. Pl. XVI; Watson 1983).

The Chinese, who were first to practise sericulture, or silk production, imitated Sasanian art even in their silk designs. To the well-known Chinese imitations of Sasanian silks preserved in Japan's Shosoin Treasury in Nara, are now added recent discoveries of patterned silks of Chinese manufacture from the vicinity of Turfan, in China's Xinjiang province, that show typically Sasanian motifs such as the pearl-framed birds embellished with neck ribbons, jewels and diadems (Pl. 39) (Schippmann 1993: 133–4; Ghirshman 1962: 330–6, fig. 445).

Sasanian court art was also a model for expressions of imperial pomp and ceremony in the West, particularly at the royal courts of late Roman and Byzantine cities, such as Constantinople and Ravenna. The elegant and lavishly coloured Byzantine mosaics from the churches of the port city of Ravenna, on the Adriatic, show the mingling of Oriental and Mediterranean concepts of imperial splendour under the emperor Justinian, shown with his queen, Theodora, and his entourage in the sixth century mosaics from the church of San

Vitale (Grabar 1967: 156–63). Another Byzantine mosaic, dated to the early sixth century, from the church of St Apollinare Nuovo in Ravenna, showing the Magi in medallion-patterned Persian trousers, is a pointed reminder of the adoption and spread of this Persian style of dress in Byzantium in Sasanian times (Widengren 1956: 257–8).

The appeal of Sasanian art in the West is amply attested by the collections of silks and silver in European church treasuries and from burials in Coptic Egypt and in Russia's Perm region. Indeed, Sasanian metalwork is most fully documented in finds from the tombs of native traders in the central Ural mountain region, north of the Caspian Sea. Vladimir Lukonin, whose memory is honoured in the present seminar series, remains a major contributor to the study of this extraordinary collection of Sasanian silver, now housed in the State Hermitage Museum in St Petersburg (Trever and Lukonin 1987).

A facet of the dynamics of trade and exchange along the Silk Road is captured in the art of Sogdiana, to which Boris Marshak devoted last year's Lukonin Memorial Lecture. Situated south of the Aral Sea, in the valleys of the Zarafshan and the middle Oxus, the present Amu Darya River, this East Iranian feudal state flourished on the Silk Road from the fifth to the eighth centuries AD. Sogdian art, which was produced for the native landed aristocracy and for merchants of oasis-states such as Samarkand and Bukhara, is most fully documented in the extensive series of murals from Penjikent, in the present-day republic of Tajikistan. Sogdian murals were painted on the walls of both public and private buildings where they served as a form of entertainment for public consumption. The murals are characterised by an elegant and eclectic artistic style adapted to the depiction of narration through sequential action, comparable to a moving picture in slow motion. Although the Sogdian narrative art shares little with the courtly style of Sasanian Iran, the Sogdians were powerfully attracted to Sasanian decorative motifs which they eagerly imitated in their art (Azarpay *et al.* 1981). Aspiration to Sasanian courtly splendour is conspicuous in the overstatement of Sasanian pearl-bordered motifs on the clothing of the Sogdian ruler of Samarkand, and in that of his retinue and visiting dignitaries, depicted in murals from Afrasiab at Samarkand, dated to the seventh century AD (Pl. 40).

3 The Significance of Sasanian Decorative Motifs

The significance of embellished animal, plant, and symbolic motifs in Sasanian art remains a subject of much speculation. Sasanian decorative arts often show symbols such as winged palmettes on pedestals, animals with extraordinary attributes, such as jewels with flying ribbons borne around their heads, necks, and bodies, and composite creatures, such as the winged horse and the dog-bird with a peacock's tail.

The Sasanian artistic style in the decorative arts is distinguished by single or repeated units of isolated motifs, or of pairs of confronted or addorsed images (Col. Pl. XVII). Animal figures are generally arranged in simple hieratic compositions against a plain background, usually framed by scroll- or pearl-borders. The ram and the winged horse on two groups of silk fragments from Antinoe, in Egypt, may be cited as examples (Col. Pls XVIII–XIX, Fig. 16). These fragments, which are now in the collections of the Louvre and the Textile Museum at Lyon, were produced in Sasanian royal workshops of the sixth and early seventh centuries, when Sasanian silk production and weaving technology were at their peak (Martiniani-Reber and Bénazeth 1997: nos. 6,60). The hieratic severity noted in the depictions of these animals is accentuated by their formal and chromatic sobriety. The majestic winged horse is embellished with a pearl-studded harness with floating ribbons and a rosette-topped crescent-shaped crown. The short ribbons tied above the knees stress the horse's conspicuously high knee flexion and its animated motion (Col. Pl. XIX, Fig. 16). The ram is portrayed with similar formal and chromatic sobriety, and with a pearl halter with floating ribbons (Col. Pl. XVIII). It is further distinguished by its regal posture, stylised body markings, a large, hooded, golden eye, and profile head embellished with a pair of great curved horns displayed in splendid frontality. These attributes describe domesticated animals that posture as the noblest of their species. A similar display of majesty and sobriety characterises the principal motif in other examples of the decorative arts produced in Sasanian workshops.

The significance of these motifs was recently re-examined by Anna Jerusalimskaya of the State Hermitage Museum (1993), who has drawn attention to their astral, cosmological and Zoroastrian implications. But a strictly religious explanation of these animals hardly accounts for their widespread use and popularity in the non-Zoroastrian world. As noted earlier in this paper, Sasanian decorative arts enjoyed considerable prestige and popularity among Iran's non-Zoroastrian contemporaries, from the Atlantic to the China Sea, in both Sasanian and Islamic times. One of the reasons for the universal appeal of Sasanian art was doubtless its courtly style which served as a model for other imperial traditions and aspiring leaderships. But Sasanian art also projects another message of universal appeal. This, I would argue, is the portrayal of the positive social and spiritual values of the ancient Iranians. Those values, which in many ways have transcended the Sasanian period, hold the universe as God's coherent and orderly creation.

The ancient Iranian world view, as reflected in the Avesta and in Pahlavi sources, portrays the supreme creator, Ahuramazda or Ohrmazd, as goodness and light, and his counterpart, Ahriman, as the quintessence of evil, darkness and deceit. God creates the world as a weapon against evil. His creations include six spiritual entities (Amahraspands) that patronise God's material creations which are the sky, water, earth, plants, animals, man, and fire (Boyce and Grenet 1991: 398; Zaehner 1956). Man's role is to cooperate with nature towards the ultimate defeat of evil by leading a life of good thoughts, good words and good deeds. The worthy man can expect to enjoy happiness and the good things of life on earth, and the 'best existence' hereafter. A remarkable ode to the glorification of material life is offered in the prayer to the deity that presides over the 25th day of the Zoroastrian month, Ahrishwang (Mahamedi 1971: 7, 192–4). The deity is asked to grant the worshipper enjoyment of 'the many gold, silver, pearls and brilliant jewels, the useful animals of many kinds and flocks.' And of 'the fruitful trees of every kind, and homes and houses with wonderful design, large and beautiful, the well-spread bedding and smart clothes, the fertile wife, a maiden with good body and good form, best chosen to the sight.' All these in addition to 'horses, sovereignty over men, the possession of thrones and cities, the possession of diadems and ornaments, of fragrance, etc.' so that he, the worshipper, 'may be the most fortunate, and the most active in the material world.'

Avestan texts emphasise the stability and prosperity of the material world and of mankind, animals, and plant life. God's weapons against evil are listed in hierarchical order, from good to best, according to their social, material and moral merit. Ingrained in the ancient Iranian psyche is not only the opposition of best and worst, but also the concept of superlatives, that which is best in all things. The concept of the best is first attested in the Gāthās, in the Old Avestan neuter plural '*vahishtā*' (yasna 28.8) which refers to the 'best things' (goods, teachings, words) of this life and the rewards of eschatology, especially paradise (Persian *behesht*). This *vahishtā* is a chief value concept and the focal form throughout the Gāthās.[2] A hierarchical order underlies classifications of abstract and physical qualities in both the spiritual and the material world. It is found, for example, in the geographical order of countries and regions on earth, as it is in the stages travelled by the soul of the deceased from earth to the realm of infinite light, in paradise. It defines social classes and their respective chromatic and physical associations, the order of moral qualities in man, and is notable in matters of Zoroastrian ritual (Duchesne-Guillemin 1966: 129–40; de Menace 1945: I, 23–5).

The best king, according to Zoroastrian conventional wisdom, is the ruler, who as head of state and guardian of religion, creates justice and order. He is also a heroic hunter and supreme warrior. The best man is he who follows his beliefs, and is truthful and respectful. The best woman is loyal, good natured, attractive and young. The best livestock is the bull with a large herd of cows. The best horse is the swiftest, the best plants are the grape, the date and wheat, the best food is milk, and the best drink is wine. When drunk in moderation, wine increases, among other things, understanding and intellect. It removes vexation and flushes the complexion. It improves memory, the senses, work and sleep. Wine is therefore a fitting drink for the celebration of special occasions such as thanksgivings and memorials (Tafazzoli 1975/76: XIV, 78–9; West 1885: 107–8; Zaehner 1956).

As expected, Zoroastrian conventional wisdom presents Ahriman's counter creations also in a hierarchical order, and lists them from bad to worst. An engaging example is the condemnation of trivial pursuits. It is considered sinful to involve oneself with useless and trivial activities. The ultimate sinner is one who actually enjoys such pursuits.

The imagery of Sasanian art gains special significance when viewed in light of the ancient Iranian world view. Thus in the decorative arts, animal motifs such as the bull, horse, ram, cock and the mythical sen, and plants, such as pomegranate and tulip, are rich in cultural, economic and religious significance. They are, moreover, celebrations of life's promise and bounty expressed as visual metaphors. It is surely God's best and most useful creations that are eulogised in Sasanian decorative arts. The brave warrior and heroic hunter, crowned and honoured (Pls 35–37), is surely the noblest king. The high-born young queen or noblewoman, carved on precious gems, is certainly the finest woman. The quintessence of swiftness, the crowned and ornately harnessed steed, wishfully supplied

16 *Left* A winged horse on a late Sasanian silk fragment from Antinoe, Egypt.

17 *Right* Detail of design on the interior of a silver-gilt bowl, formerly in the Foroughi collection, showing dancing women in association with vintaging scenes.

with wings, is clearly the best mount (Col. Pl. XIX, Fig. 16) The ultimate symbols of material bounty, cattle and sheep, embellished and opulently haltered, are the best of animals (Col. Pl. XVIII). The versatile grape is the choicest fruit, and the exhilarating and beneficial wine an unparalleled drink (Pl. 41). Finally, the blossoming tree and the vine harvest, as allusions to the promise of spring and the bounty of autumn, are clearly symbols of the best of seasons (Fig. 17).

These considerations lead me to explain the thematic content of Sasanian art as generic, with a collective significance that invariably embraces and overrides its specific, historical or narrative meaning. Thus Sasanian decorative motifs, such as embellished birds, animals and plants, and allegorical themes such as the royal hunt may be read as visual metaphors that encapsulate ancient Iranian and Zoroastrian socio-religious ideas.

The spread of Sasanian art beyond the Persian world occurred at a time when ardent missionaries promoted their proselytising religions through Buddhist, Christian, and Manichaean scriptures and by means of their religious arts. But the national creed of the Sasanians did not encourage converts and its tenets were reserved for Zoroastrian believers. Nevertheless, their cultural patterns were effectively packaged in Sasanian art. Thus the spread of Sasanian art beyond the Persian world may be traced not only to that art's courtly overtones, but also to its positive message, a message that projects the prevailing ancient Iranian values in the universal language of art.

Notes

1 On the left wall of the large grotto is a relief that shows the Qajar governor of Kermanshah, Mohammad Ali Mirza Dowlat Shah, son of Fath Ali Shah, and his two sons, dated to 1822 (Curtis, J.E., 1989: fig. 85).

2 I wish to thank Martin Schwartz for providing me with this reference, and for his comments on the Gāthic concept of *vahishtā*. See also Gāthās, Yasnas 30.2, 31.1, 34.15, 45.4, 45.5, 45.6, 50.5, *passim*.

Bibliography

Adams, R.Mc.C., 1965. *Land behind Baghdad. A History of Settlement on the Diyala Plains*, Chicago and London.

Adams, R.Mc.C., 1981. *Heartland of Cities. Surveys of Ancient Settlement and Land Use on the Central Floodplain of the Euphrates*, Chicago and London.

Adams, R.Mc.C., 1970. 'Tell Abu Sarifa. A Sassanian-Islamic ceramic sequence from south central Iraq', *Ars Orientalis* 8: 87–119.

Aggoula, B., 1985. 'Inscriptions et graffites araméens d'Assour', supplement 43 to *Annali di Napoli*.

Aghion, I., and Avisseau-Broustet, M., 1994. 'Le duc de Luynes, archéologue, historien, homme de sciences et collectionneur', *Revue de la Bibliothèque Nationale de France* 3:12–20.

Amiet, P., 1967. 'Nouvelles acquisitions – Musée du Louvre, Département des antiquités orientales; Antiquités parthes et sassanides', *Revue du Louvre* 17: 273–82.

Amiet, P., 1988. *Suse: 6000 ans d'histoire*, Paris.

Andrae, W., and Lenzen, H., 1933. *Die Partherstadt Assur*, Wissenschaftliche Veröffentlichungen der Deutschen Orient-Gesellschaft 57, Berlin.

Apakidze, A.M., *et al.*, 1958. *Mtskheta* I, Tbilisi.

Artamonov, M.I., 1969. *Treasures from Scythian Tombs*, London.

Augé, C., Curiel, R., and Le Rider, G., 1979. *Terrasses sacrées de Bard-è Néchandeh et Masjid-i Solaiman. Les trouvailles monetaires*, Mémoires de la Délégation Archéologique en Iran 44, Paris.

Azarnoush, M., 1994. *The Sasanian Manor House at Hajiabad*, Mesopotamia III, Florence.

Azarpay, G., Belenitskii, A.M., and Marshak, B.I., 1981. *Sogdian Painting. The Pictorial Epic in Oriental Art*, Berkeley, Los Angeles and London.

Babelon, E., 1990. *Guide illustré au Cabinet des Médailles et Antiques de la Bibliothèque Nationale*, Paris.

Balcer, J.M., 1978. 'Excavations at Tal-i Malyan: Part 2, Parthian and Sasanian coins and burials (1976)', *Iran* 16: 86–92.

Beyer, K., 1998. *Die aramäischen Inschriften aus Assur, Hatra und dem übrigen Ostmesopotamien*, Göttingen.

Bivar, A.D.H., 1969. *Catalogue of the Western Asiatic Seals in the British Museum. Stamp Seals II, The Sassanian Dynasty*, London.

Boucharlat, R., 1998. 'À la recherche d'Ecbatane sur Tepe Hegmataneh', *Iranica Antiqua* 33: 173–86.

Boyce, M., and Grenet, F., 1991. *A History of Zoroastrianism III*, Handbuch der Orientalistik I. VIII.1.2.2.3, Leiden.

Burnes, Lt. Col. Sir Alexander, 1842. *Cabool*, London.

Byron, R., 1937. *The Road to Oxiana*, London.

Chabouillet, M., 1858. *Catalogue général et raisonné des camées et pierres gravées de la Bibliothèque Impériale*, Paris.

Chase, W.T., 1968. 'The technical examination of two Sasanian silver plates', *Ars Orientalis* 7: 75–93.

Chelkowski, P., 1989. 'Narrative painting and painting recitation in Qajar Iran', *Muqarnas* 6: 98–111.

Christensen, A., 1936. *L'Iran sous les sassanides*, Copenhagen.

Cohen, A., 1937. *Everyman's Talmud*, London.

Colledge, M.A.R., 1976. *The Art of Palmyra*, London.

Colledge, M.A.R., 1977. *Parthian Art*, London.

Collon, D., 1995. *Ancient Near Eastern Art*, London.

Craddock, P., Lang, J., and Simpson, St. J., in press. 'New evidence for crucible steel', *Journal of Historical Metallurgy*.

Cumont, F., 1926. *Fouilles de Doura-Europos*, Paris.

Cunningham, Alexander, 1841. 'A sketch of the second silver plate found at Badakshân', *Journal of the Asiatic Society of Bengal*: 570–2.

Curtis, J.E., Green, A.R., and Knight, W., 1987–8. 'Preliminary report on excavations at Tell Deir Situn and Grai Darki', *Sumer* 45: 49–53.

Curtis, J.E., 1989. *Ancient Persia*, London.

Curtis, J.E., 1993. 'William Kennet Loftus and his excavations at Susa', *Iranica Antiqua* 28: 1–55.

Curtis, J. E., 1997a. 'Franks and the Oxus Treasure', in Caygill, M., and Cherry, J. (eds), *A.W. Franks*, London: 232–49.

Curtis, J.E., 1997b. 'The church at Khirbet Deir Situn', *Al-Rafidan* 18: 369–85.

Curtis, V.S., 1993a. 'A Parthian statuette from Susa and the bronze statue from Shami', *Iran* 31: 63–9.

Curtis, V.S., 1993 b. *Persian Myths*, London.

Curtis, V.S., 1996. 'Parthian and Sasanian furniture', in Herrmann, G. (ed.), *The Furniture of Western Asia, Ancient and Traditional*, Mainz: 233–44.

Curtis, V.S., and Simpson, St. J., 1997. 'Archaeological news from Iran', *Iran* 35: 137–44.

Curtis, V.S., and Simpson, St. J., 1998.

'Archaeological news from Iran: seond report', *Iran* 36: 185–94.

Dalton, O.M., 1909. 'On a Persian silver dish of the fourth century', *Archaeologia* 61: 381–2.

Dalton, O.M., 1964. *The Treasure of the Oxus with other Examples of Early Oriental Metalwork*, 3rd edition, London.

de Menace, P.J., 1945. *Shikand-Gumānī Vazār (translation and commentary)*, Collectanea Friburgensia 30, Fribourg en Suisse.

Debevoise, N.C., 1969. *A Political History of Parthia*, 2nd ed., Chicago and London.

Delaporte, L., 1926. 'Une coupe sassanide de Bahram Gour', *Arethuse* 3: 143–8.

Dimand, M.S., 1959. 'A group of Sasanian silver bowls', *Aus der Welt der Islamischen Kunst. Festschrift für Ernst Kühnel*, Berlin: 11–14.

Dodgeon, M.H., and Lieu, S.N.C. (eds.), 1991. *The Roman Eastern Frontier and the Persian Wars* (AD 226–363). *A Documentary History*, London and New York.

Downey, S.B., 1977. *The Excavations at Dura-Europos. Final Report III, Part I, Fasc.2: The Stone and Plaster Sculpture*, Los Angeles.

Duchesne-Guillemin, J., 1966. *Symbols and Values in Zoroastrianism. Their Survival and Renewal*, New York.

Dürr, N. 1967. 'Une nouvelle carafe sassanide', *Genava* n.s. 15: 25–41.

Erdmann, K., 1936. 'Die sasanidischen Jagdschalen', *Jahrbuch der preussischen Kunstsammlungen* 57: 193–231.

Erdmann, K., 1937. 'Das Datum des Taqi Bustan', *Ars Islamica* 4: 79–97.

Erdmann, K., 1943. 'Zur Chronologie der sasanidischen 'Jagdschalen' ', *Zeitschrift der deutschen morgenländischen Gesellschaft* 7: 239–83.

Fajans, S., 1957. 'Recent Russian literature on newly found Middle Eastern metal vessels', *Ars Orientalis* 2: 55–76.

Fiey, J.-M., 1959. *Mossoul chretienne*, Beirut.

Fiey, J.-M., 1965. *Assyrie chretienne*, 2 vols., Beirut.

Flandin, E., and Coste, P., 1843–54. *Voyage en Perse*, 5 vols, Paris.

Frye, R.N., 1972. 'Byzantine and Sasanian trade relations with Northeast Russia', *Dumbarton Oaks Papers* 26: 263–9.

Frye, R.N., 1984. *The History of Ancient Iran*, Munich.

Fukai, S., and Horiuchi, H., 1969–84. *Taq-i Bustan* I-IV, Tokyo.

Fukai, S., 1977. *Persian Glass*, New York, Tokyo and Kyoto.

Gabutti-Roncalli, A., 1996. 'The Italian excavations in Old Nisa: the northern corner of the Round Hall complex', *Mesopotamia* 31: 161–77.

Ghirshman, R., 1962. *Iran. Parthians and Sassanians*, London.

Ghirshman, R., 1976. *Terrasses sacrées de Bard-è Néchandeh et Masjid-i Solaiman*, 2 vols., Mémoires de la Délégation Archéologique en Iran 45, Paris.

Gibson, M.G., 1972. *The City and Area of Kish*, Miami.

Göbl, R., 1971. *Sasanian Numismatics*, Braunschweig.

Godard, Y., 1938a. 'Bouteille d'argent sasanide', *Āthār-é Īrān* 3: 291–300.

Godard, Y., 1938b. 'Plat d'argent découvert près de Kazwin', *Āthār-é Īrān* 3: 300–6.

Gorelick, L., and Gwinnett, A.J., 1990. 'The Ancient Near Eastern cylinder seal as social emblem and status symbol', *Journal of Near Eastern Studies* 49: 45–56.

Grabar, A., 1967. *The Golden Age of Justinian*, New York.

Grayson, A.K., 1976. *Assyrian Royal Inscriptions 2*, Wiesbaden.

Grignaschi, M., 1966. 'Quelques spécimens de la littérature sassanide conservés dans les bibliothèques d'Istanbul', *Journal Asiatique* 254: 1–142.

Gropp, G., 1968. 'Die parthische Inschrift von Sar-Pol-e Zohab', *Zeitschrift der Deutschen Morgenländischen Gesellschaft* 118: 315–19.

Gunter, A.C., and Jett, P., 1992. *Ancient Iranian Metalwork in the Arthur M. Sackler Gallery and the Freer Gallery of Art*, Washington, D.C.

Gyselen, R., 1989. *La géographie administrative de l'empire sassanide*, Res Orientales 1, Bures-sur-Yvette.

Hamilton, R.W., 1953. 'Carved plaster in Umayyad architecture', *Iraq* 15: 43–55.

Harper, P.O., et al., 1978. *The Royal Hunter. Art of the Sasanian Empire*, New York.

Harper, P.O., and Meyers, P., 1981. *Silver Vessels of the Sasanian Period I: Royal Imagery*, New York.

Heinrich, E., 1935. *VI vorläufiger Bericht über. . .Uruk-Warka*, Berlin.

Herrmann, G., 1977. *The Iranian Revival*, Oxford.

Herrmann, G., 1983. *The Sasanian Rock Reliefs at Bishapur* Part 3, Iranische Denkmäler 11/II, Berlin.

Herrmann, G., 1989. 'The Art of the Sasanians', in Ferrier, R.W. (ed.), *The Arts of Persia*, New Haven and London: 61–79.

Herrmann, G., and Kurbansakhatov, K., et al., 1995. 'The International Merv Project. Preliminary report on the third season (1994)', *Iran* 33: 31–60.

Herrmann, G., Kurbansakhatov, K., and Simpson, St J., 1997. 'The International Merv Project. Preliminary report on the fifth season (1996)', *Iran* 35: 1–33.

Herzfeld, E., 1920. *Am Tor von Asien*, Berlin.

Herzfeld, E., 1932. 'Sakastan. . .Die Lehnsfürsten unter den Nachfolgern Mithradates II', *Archaeologische Mitteilungen aus Iran* 4: 45–85.

Herzfeld, E., 1938. 'Khusrau Parwēz und der Taq-ī Vastan', *Archaeologische Mitteilungen aus Iran* 9: 91–158.

Herzfeld, E.E., 1941. *Iran in the Ancient East*, London and New York.

Hinz, W., 1969. *Altiranische Funde und Forschungen*, Berlin.

Hitti, P.K., 1916. *The Origins of the Islamic State, being a translation from the Arabic, etc.*, New York.

Hobbs, R., 1995. 'Roman coins from Merv, Turkmenistan', *Oxford Journal of Archaeology* 14: 97–102.

Howard-Johnston, J., 1995. 'The two great powers in late antiquity: a comparison', in Cameron, A. (ed.), *The Byzantine and Early Islamic Near East III*, Princeton: 157–226.

Humbach, H., and Skjaervø, P.O., 1978–83. *The Sasanian Inscription of Paikuli*, 3 vols, Wiesbaden.

Invernizzi, A., 1968–9. 'A relief in the style of the Gandhara School from Choche', *Mesopotamia* 3–4: 145–58.
Invernizzi, A., 1994. 'Die hellenistischen Grundlagen der parthischen Kunst', *Archaeologische Mitteilungen aus Iran* 27: 191–203.
Jerusalimskaya, A., 1993. 'Soieries sassanides', in *Splendeur des Sasanides*, catalogue of exhibition at Musées royaux d'Art et d'Histoire, Brussels: 113–20.
Karvonen-Kannas, K., 1995. *The Seleucid and Parthian Terracotta Figurines from Babylon*, Florence.
Kawami, T., 1987. *Monumental Art of the Parthian Period*, Acta Iranica 26, Leiden.
Keall, E.J., 1974. 'Some thoughts on the early eyvan', in *Near Eastern Numismatics, Iconography, Epigraphy and History. Studies in Honor of George C. Miles*, Beirut: 123–30.
Keall, E.J., 1975. 'Parthian Nippur and Vologases' southern strategy: an hypothesis', *Journal of the American Oriental Society* 95: 620–32.
Keall, E.J., 1982. 'Qal'eh Yazdigird. An overview of the monumental architecture', *Iran* 20: 51–72.
Keall, E.J., 1989. 'The Art of the Parthians', in Ferrier, R.W. (ed.), *The Arts of Persia*, New Haven and London: 49–59.
Kessler, K.H., 1984. 'Eine arsakidenzeitliche Urkunde aus Warka', *Baghdader Mitteilungen* 15: 273–81.
King, G.R.D., 1997. 'A Nestorian monastic settlement on the island of Sir Bani Yas, Abu Dhabi: a preliminary report', *Bulletin of the School of Oriental and African Studies* 60: 221–35.
Koldewey, R., 1914. *The Excavations at Babylon*, London.
Koshelenko, G., Lapshin, A., and Novikov, S., 1989. 'Mansur Depe excavations', *Bulletin of the Asia Institute* ns 3: 45–52.
Kraeling, C.H., 1956. *The Excavations at Dura Europos. Final Report VIII, Part 1: The Synagogue*, New Haven.
Kröger, J., 1979. 'Sasanian Iran and India: questions of interaction', in Hartel, H. (ed.), *South Asian Archaeology 1979*: 441–8.
Kröger, J., 1982. *Sasanidischer Stuckdecor*, Baghdader Forschungen 5, Mainz.
Kuhrt, A., and Sherwin-White, S. (eds), 1987. *Hellenism in the East*, London.
Lamm, C.J., 1937. *Cotton in Mediaeval Textiles of the Near East*, Paris.
Laufer, B., 1919. *Sino-Iranica*, Chicago.
Lerner, J.A., 1980. 'Three Achaemenid "fakes"', *Expedition* 22/2: 5–16.
Leshchenko, V.Iu., 1971. *Vostochnie Klady na Urale v VII-XIII vv*, Leningrad.
Leshchenko, V.Iu., 1976. 'Ispolzovanie vostochnogo serebra na Urale', in Darkevich, V.P., *Khudozhestvennii Metall Vostoka*, Moscow: 176–89.
Levit–Tawil, D., 1993. 'Re-dating the Sasanian reliefs at Tang-e Qandil and Barm-e Dilak: composition and style as dating criteria', *Iranica Antiqua* 28: 141–68.
Levy, R. (transl.), 1985. *The Epic of the Kings*, London.
Lukonin, V., 1968. 'Monnaie d'Ardashir I et l'art officiel sassanide', *Iranica Antiqua* 8: 106–17.
Luschey, H., 1968. 'Der Löwe von Ekbatana', *Archaeologische Mitteilungen aus Iran* ns 1: 115–22.
Lynton, N., 1997. Review of A. Blühm *et al.*, *The Colour of Sculpture 1840–1910* (Amsterdam 1996), in *The Art Book* 4, part 3: 6–7.
Mahamedi, H., 1971. *Propitiations to the Thirty Deities of Zoroastrianism: the Pahlavi Text Stäyishn i Si Rözag*, Ph.D. thesis, Harvard University.
Martiniani-Reber, M., and Bénazeth, D., 1997. *Textiles et Mode Sassanides. Les Tissus orientaux conservés au Département des Antiquités égyptiennes*, Musée du Louvre, Paris.
Masson, M.E., and Pugachenkova, G.A., 1956. *Parthyanskie Ritoni Nisi*, Moscow.
Matthiesen, H.E., 1992. *Sculpture in the Parthian Period*, 2 vols, Aarhus.
Mehrkiyan, J., 1997. 'The Elymaian rock-carving of Shaivand, Izeh', *Iran* 35: 67–72.
Miller, R.A., 1959. *Accounts of Western Nations in the History of the Northern Chou Dynasty*, Berkeley and Los Angeles.
Morey, C.R., 1937. 'Art of the Dark Ages: a unique show', *The Art News* [20 Feb]: 9–16, 24.
Mørkholm, O., 1991. *Early Hellenistic Coinage*, Cambridge.
Morony, M.G., 1984. *Iraq after the Muslim Conquest*, Princeton.
Movassat, J.D., 1988. *The Large Vault at Taq-i Bustan: A Study in Late Sassanian Royal Art*, Ph.D. thesis, University of California, Berkeley.
Naveh, J., and Shaked, S., 1993. *Magic Spells and Formulae. Aramaic Incantations of Late Antiquity*, Jerusalem.
Newman, J., 1932. *The Agricultural Life of the Jews in Babylonia between the Years 200 CE-500 CE*, London.
Oates, D. and J., 1958. 'Nimrud 1957: The Hellenistic Settlement', *Iraq* 20: 114–57.
Okada, Y., 1992. ''Ain Shai'a and the early Gulf churches: an architectural analogy', *Al-Rafidan* 13: 87–93.
Oppenheimer, A., 1983. *Babylonian Judaica in the Talmudic Period*, Wiesbaden.
Orbeli, J.A., and Trever, K.V., 1935. *Sasanidskii Metall*, Moscow and Leningrad.
Orbeli, J. A., 1938. 'Sasanian and early Islamic metalwork', *A Survey of Persian Art* I, London and New York: 716–70.
Overlaet, B.J., 1982. 'Contribution to Sasanian armament in connection with a decorated helmet', *Iranica Antiqua* 17: 189–206.
Overlaet, B., 1993. 'Organisation militaire et armement', in *Splendeur des Sasanides*, catalogue of exhibition at Musées royaux d'Art et d'Histoire, Brussels: 89–94.
Perkins, A., 1973. *The Art of Dura-Europos*, Oxford.
Philipko, V.N., 1991. 'Una testa con elmo da Nisa Vecchia', *Mesopotamia* 26: 155–64.
Pope, A.U. (ed.), 1938. *A Survey of Persian Art* IV, London and New York.
Quarantelli, E., 1985 (ed.). *The Land between Two Rivers. Twenty Years of Italian Archaeology in the Middle East. The Treasures of Mesopotamia*, Turin.
Rahbar, M., 1999. 'Khorheh: une résidence parthe

sur le plateau iranien', *Dossiers de l'Archéologie* 243: 44–6.
Reade, J.E., 1998. 'Greco-Parthian Nineveh', *Iraq* 60: 65–83.
Reitlinger, G., 1963. *The Economics of Taste* II, London.
Roaf, M., 1984. 'Excavations at Tell Mohammed 'Arab in the Eski Mosul Dam Salvage Project', *Iraq* 46: 141–56.
Roaf, M., 1989. 'The Art of the Achaemenians', in Ferrier, R.W. (ed.), *The Arts of Persia*, New Haven and London: 26–47.
Robin, C., *et al.*, 1997. *Yémen au pays de la reine de Saba*, Paris.
Safar, F., and Mustafa, M.A., 1974. *Hatra. The City of the Sun God*, Baghdad.
Sarraf. M.R., 1997. 'Neue architektonische und städtebauliche Funde von Ekbatana-Tepe (Hamadan)', *Archäologische Mitteilungen aus Iran und Turan* 29: 321–39.
Schippmann, K., 1993. 'L'influence de la culture sassanide', in *Splendeur des Sassanides*, catalogue of exhibition at Musées royaux d'Art et d'Histoire, Brussels: 131–40.
Schmidt, J., 1972. *XXVI und XXVII vorlaüfiger Bericht über...Uruk-Warka*, Berlin.
Sedov, A.V., 1992. 'New archaeological and epigraphical material from Qana (South Arabia)', *Arabian Archaeology and Epigraphy* 3: 110–37.
Sellwood, D., 1980. *An Introduction to the Coinage of Parthia*, 2nd rev. edition, London.
Shahbazi, A.S., 1990. 'Byzantine-Iranian relations', *Encylopaedia Iranica* IV: 588–99.
Shalem, A., 1994. 'The fall of al-Madā'in: some literary references concerning Sasanian spoils of war in mediaeval Islamic treasuries', *Iran* 32: 77–81.
Sherwin-White, S.M., 1984. 'Shami, the Seleucids and dynastic cult: a note', *Iran* 22: 160–1.
Sherwin-White, S., and Kuhrt, A., 1993. *From Samarkhand to Sardis. A new approach to the Seleucid empire*, London.
Simpson, St J., 1996. 'From Tekrit to the Jaghjagh: Sasanian sites, settlement patterns and material culture in Northern Mesopotamia', in Bartl, K., and Hauser, S.R. (eds), *Continuity and Change in Northern Mesopotamia from the Hellenistic to the Early Islamic period*, Berlin: 87–126.
Simpson, St J., 1997a. 'Ctesiphon', in Meyers, E.M. (ed.), *The Oxford Encyclopedia of Archaeology in the Near East* I: 77–9.
Simpson, St J., 1997b. 'Partho-Sasanian ceramic industries in Mesopotamia', in Freestone, I., and Gaimster, D. (eds), *Pottery in the Making : World Ceramic Traditions*, London: 74–9.
Simpson, St J., 1998. 'Gilt-silver and clay: a Late Sasanian skeuomorphic pitcher from Iran', *Entlang der Seidenstrasse. Frühmittelalterliche Kunst zwischen Persien und China in der Abegg-Stiftung*, Riggisberg: 335–44.
Smirnov, Ia. I., 1909. *Vostochnoe Serebro*, St Petersburg.
Smith, M.C., and Wright, H.T., 1988. 'The ceramics from Ras Hafun in Somalia: notes on a classical maritime site', *Azania* 23: 115–41.
Stein, A., 1940. *Old Routes of Western Iran*, London.
Stronach, D., 1978. *Pasargadae: a Report on the Excavations conducted by the British Institute of Persian Studies from 1961 to 1963*, Oxford.
Tafazzoli, A., 1974. 'A list of trades and crafts in the Sassanian period', *Archaeologische Mitteilungen aus Iran* n.s. 7: 191–6.
Tafazzoli, A., 1975/76. *Mēnōg i Khrad*, translation and commentary, Tehran (in Persian).
Thierry, F., 1993. 'Sur les monnaies sassanides trouvées en Chine', *Res Orientales V: Circulation des monnaies, des marchandises et des biens*, Bures-sur-Yvette: 89–139.
Trever, K.V., and Lukonin, V.G., 1987. *Sasanidiskoe Serebro*, Moscow.
Trever, K.V., 1952. 'K voprosu o tak nazyvaemykh sasanidskikh pamiatnikakh', *Sovietskaya Arkheologiya* 16: 282–8.
Trümpelmann, L., 1977. *Sarpol-i Zohab: Die Felsreliefs I-IV, Das Parthische Felsrelief*, Iranische Denkmäler 7, Berlin.
Vanden Berghe, L., 1959. *Archéologie de l'Iran Ancien*, Leiden.
Vanden Berghe, L., 1983. *Reliefs Rupestres de l'Iran Ancien*, Brussels.
Vanden Berghe, L., and Schippmann, K., 1985. *Les Reliefs Rupestres d'Elymaïde (Iran) de l'époque Parthe*, Gent.
Vanden Berghe, L., 1993. 'La Sculpture', in *Splendeur des Sassanides*, catalogue of exhibition at Musées royaux d'Art et d'Histoire, Brussels: 71–88.
Vogelsang-Eastwood, G.M., 1988. '*Zilu* Carpets from Iran', *Studia Iranica* 17: 225–40.
Vollmer, J.E., Keall, E.J., and Nagai-Berthrong, E., 1983. *Silk Roads. China Ships*, Catalogue of an exhibition at the Royal Ontario Museum, Toronto.
Watson, W., 1983. 'Iran and China,' *The Cambridge History of Iran* 3 (1), Cambridge: 537–58.
Wenke, R.J., 1975–6. 'Imperial investments and agricultural developments in Parthian and Sasanian Khuzestan: 150 BC to AD 640', *Mesopotamia* 10–11: 31–221.
West, E.W., 1885. *Pahalvi Texts* III, Oxford 1885.
Whitcomb, D.S., 1985. *Before the Roses and Nightingales. Excavations at Qasr-i Abu Nasr, Old Shiraz*, New York.
Widengren, G., 1956. 'Some remarks on riding costume and articles of dress among Iranian peoples in antiquity', *Studia Ethnographica Upsaliensia* 11: 228–76.
Wiesehöfer, J., 1996. *Ancient Persia*, London.
Wigram, W.A., 1929. *The Assyrians and their Neighbours*, London.
Williams, R.G., and Boyd, J.W., 1993. *Ritual Art and Knowledge. Aesthetic Theory and Zoroastrian Ritual*, Columbia, South Carolina.
Wroth, W.W., 1903. *Catalogue of the Coins of Parthia (in the British Museum)*, London.
Yamauchi, E.M., 1967. *Mandaic Incantation Texts*, New Haven.
Zaehner, R.C., 1956. *The Teachings of the Magi: a Compendium of Zoroastrian Beliefs*, London and New York.
Ziegler, C., 1962. *Die Terrakotten von Warka*, Berlin.

Illustration Acknowledgments

BM = Photography copyright The British Museum

Figures
1 Photo BM.
2 Photo BM.
3 Photo BM.
4 Photo BM.
5 Map drawn by Ann Searight.
6 Map drawn by Ann Searight.
7 From Colledge 1977: fig. 39B.
8 Drawing by Tessa Rickard.
9 From Perkins 1973: pl. 14.
10 From Flandin and Coste 1843-54: IV, pl. 172.
11 Drawing by Rosalind Caldecott.
12 After Adams 1965, 1981 and Gibson 1972.
13 After Quarantelli 1985 (ed.): fig. on p. 88.
14 After Quarantelli 1985 (ed.): fig. on p. 101.
15 From Flandin and Coste 1849–54: I, pl. 8.
16 Drawing by S. Ghanimati.
17 Courtesy of G. Azarpay.

Black and white plates
1 Photo BM.
2 Photo V.S. Curtis.
3 Photo Musée du Louvre.
4 Photo Deutsche Orient Gesellschaft.
5 Photo E.J. Keall.
6 BM 92231.
7 BM 91786.
8 BM 124097.
9 From Safar and Mustafa 1974: pl. 197.
10 Photo J.E. Curtis.
11 Photo L. Vanden Berghe.
12 Photo BM.
13 Photo G. Herrmann.
14 Photo G. Herrmann.
15 Photo L. Vanden Berghe.
16 Photo L. Vanden Berghe.
17 Photo Bibliothèque Nationale.
18 Photo Bibliothèque Nationale.
19 Photo Bibliothèque Nationale.
20 Photo Museum für Islamische Kunst, Berlin.
21 BM 124094.
22 BM 1963-12-10, 3.
23 BM 124092.
24 Photo the Iranian Centre for Archaeological Research.
25 Photo Walters Art Gallery.
26 Photo Walters Art Gallery.
27 Photo Metropolitan Museum of Art.
28 Photo Freer Gallery of Art.
29 From Smirnov 1909: pl. 34, no. 62.
30 BM 119970.
31 BM 136204.
32 Photo courtesy of Gertrude Bell Photographic Archive.
33 BM 13573 + 135747.
34 BM N1806.
35 From Vanden Berghe 1993: fig. 59.
36 BM 124091.
37 Photo Bibliothèque Nationale.
38 From Ghirshman 1962: fig. 272.
39 S. 1987.33. Photo courtesy of the Arthur M. Sackler Gallery, the Freer Gallery of Art, Smithsonian Institution, Washington DC.
40 Courtesy of G. Azarpay.
41 Courtesy of G. Azarpay.

Colour plates
I Photo Dr. Harriet Crawford.
II BM 92006.
III Photo J.E. Curtis.
IV Photo J.E. Curtis.
V Photo G. Herrmann.
VI Photo G. Herrmann.
VII Photo G. Herrmann.
VIII Photo G. Herrmann.
IX BM 124095.
X BM 124091.
XI BM 119703.
XII BM 92394B.
XIII BM 91498A.
XIV Photo Musée du Louvre.
XV Photo Xsian Cultural Relics Administration.
XVI Photo Xsian Cultural Relics Administration
XVII Photo Musée du Louvre.
XVIII Photo Musée du Louvre.
XIX Photo Musée du Louvre.

PLATES

1 Coins of Arsaces II (?) (a); Mithradates I (b-e); Artabanus I (f); Mithradates II (g-i); Phraates IV (j); Artabanus IV (k); Kamnaskires III (l); Orodes II (m); and Gordian III and Abgar (n-o).

81

PLATES

2 *(left)* Ivory rhyton from Old Nisa, in the Historical Museum, Ashkhabad.

3 *(below left)* Lower part of a marble sculpture from Susa, in the Muzeh Melli, Tehran

4 *(below)* Limestone stela from Ashur, in the Archaeological Museum, Istanbul.

5 *(below right)* Stucco decoration from Qaleh-i Yazdigird showing a male figure wearing a pointed hat, tunic and trousers.

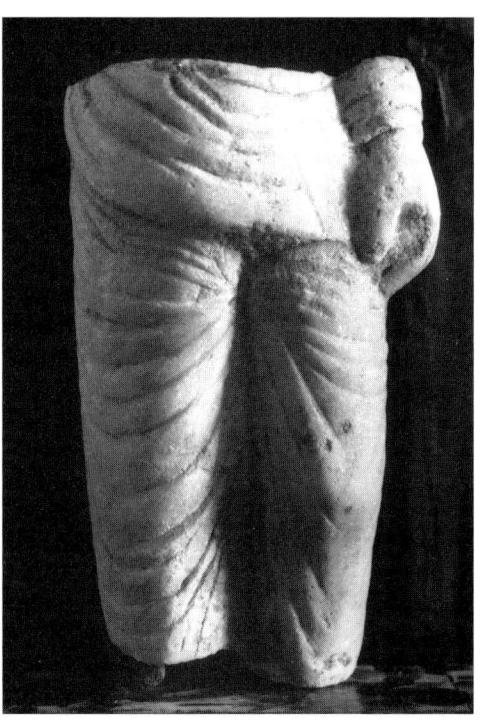

PLATES

6 *(left)* Stucco column capital from Warka, in the British Museum.

7 *(middle left)* Terracotta figurine from Warka, in the British Museum, showing a banqueter dressed in Parthian costume.

8 *(bottom left)* Gold belt clasp allegedly from the Nahavand area, in the British Museum.

9 *(below)* Statue of Atalu from Hatra.

83

PLATES

10 Relief from Susa showing Artabanus IV, in the Muzeh Melli, Tehran.

11 Rock reliefs at Tang-i Sarvak in Elymais.

12 Coins of Papak and Ardashir I (a), Ardashir I (b) and Ardashir I and his son Shapur (c).

13 Detail from jousting scene at Firuzabad showing Ardashir.

14 Horses depicted on a Sasanian relief (III) at Bishapur.

15 Detail from relief of Bahram II at Naqsh-i Rustam showing Kartir.

16 Back wall of large grotto at Taq-i Bustan showing investiture, probably of Khusro II.

17 Silver plate, in the Bibliothèque Nationale, Paris, showing a king hunting animals.

18 Silver plate, in the Bibliothèque Nationale, Paris, showing ceremonial scenes.

19 Silver ewer, in the Bibliothèque Nationale, Paris, showing crossed-over lions.

20 Silver vase, in the Museum für Islamische Kunst, Berlin, illustrated with herons and trees.

PLATES

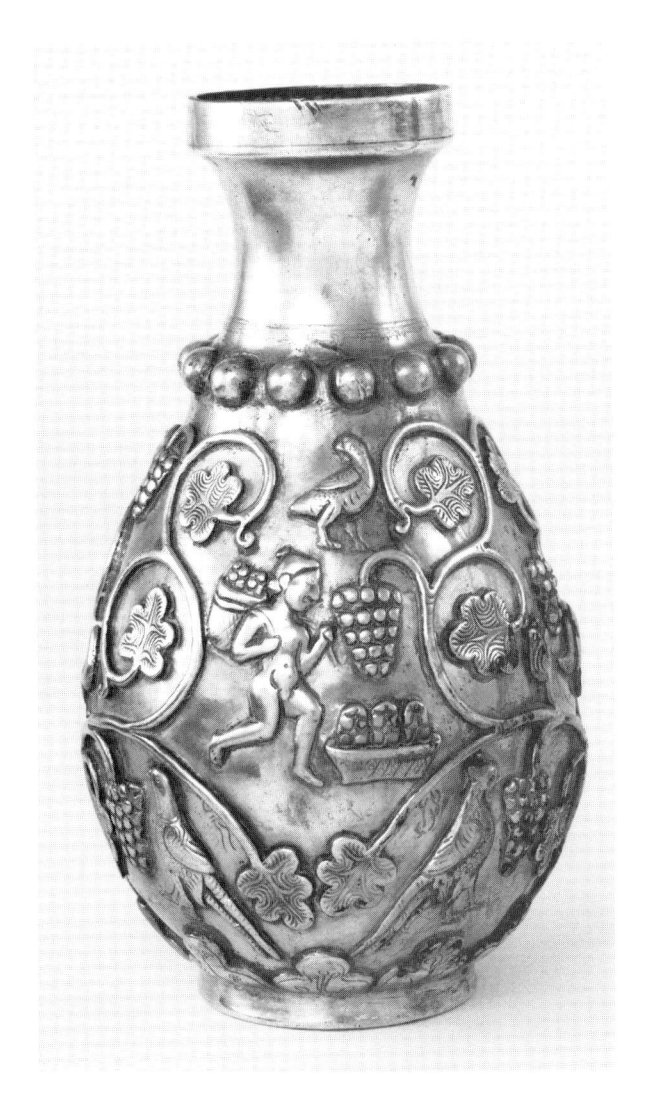

21 Silver vase, in the British Museum, decorated with vintaging scenes.

22 Silver plate, in the British Museum, showing a banqueting scene.

23 Silver plate, in the British Museum, decorated with a scene of a king hunting lions.

PLATES

24 Silver vase, in the Muzeh Melli, Tehran, decorated with dancing female figures.

26 Silver bowl, in the Walters Art Gallery, Baltimore, showing a seated king and queen.

25 Silver bowl, in the Walters Art Gallery, Baltimore, decorated with entertainment scenes and dancing females.

PLATES

27 Silver plate, in the Metropolitan Museum of Art, showing a king hunting rams.

28 Silver plate, in the Freer Gallery of Art, showing a king hunting boars.

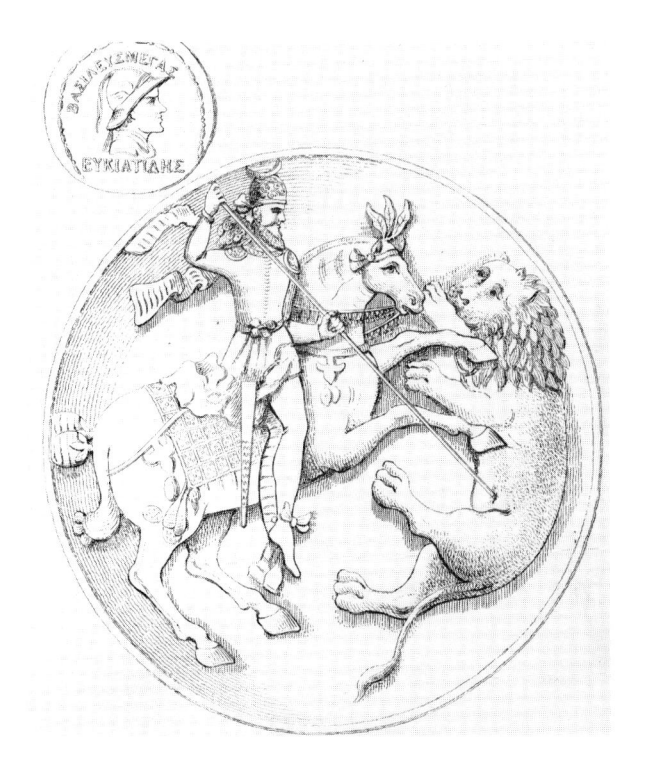

29 Drawing of a silver plate, now lost, decorated with a hunting scene.

30 Sasanian stamp seal in the British Museum giving the title 'accountant of Garmekan and Nodh-Ardashirakan' in Middle Persian.

91

31 An inscribed 'incantation bowl' in the British Museum depicting a symbolically chained Lilith in the centre.

32 The facade of the Taq-i Kisra at Ctesiphon as photographed by Gertrude Bell.

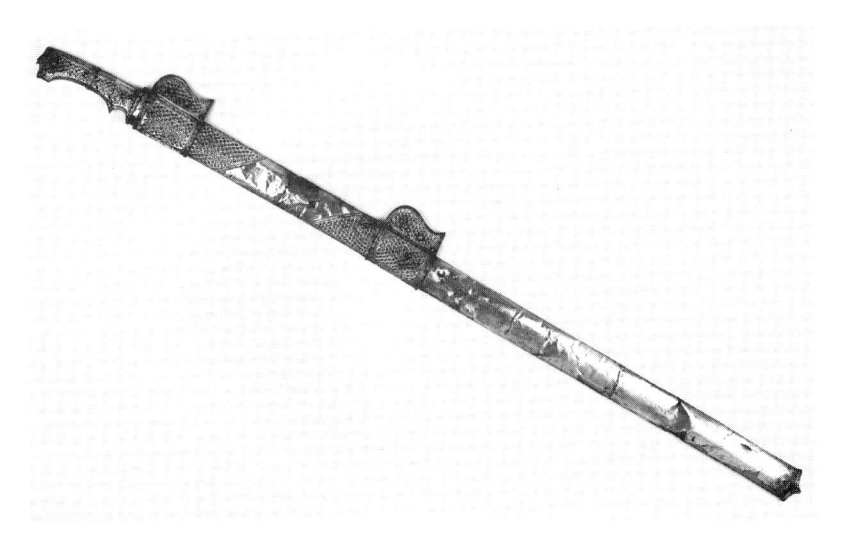

33 Sasanian sword in the British Museum with silver scabbard and crucible steel blade.

34 Stamp impression on a fragmentary Late Sasanian jar excavated at Nineveh, now in the British Museum, showing a stag with a neck-ribbon and a cross.

35 Relief showing the investiture of Ardashir I at Naqshi-i Rustam.

36 Detail from the 'Cup of Solomon', in the Cabinet des Medailles, Bibliothèque Nationale, Paris.

37 Pattern showing a *sen-murv* on the robe of Khusro II at Taq-i Bustan.

38 Horn rhyton with gazelle protome, in gilt-silver, in the Arthur M. Sackler Gallery. Height 15.5 cm.

39 Pearl-framed bird motif from a Chinese silk fragment, from the vicinity of Turfan, in Xinjiang, China.

40 Drawing showing the king of Samarkand and a member of his retinue on a seventh-century mural from a Sogdian palace complex at Afrasiab, Samarkand.

41 Sasanian stucco relief, showing a grape-vine with grape cluster, Tepe-i Mil, Iran.

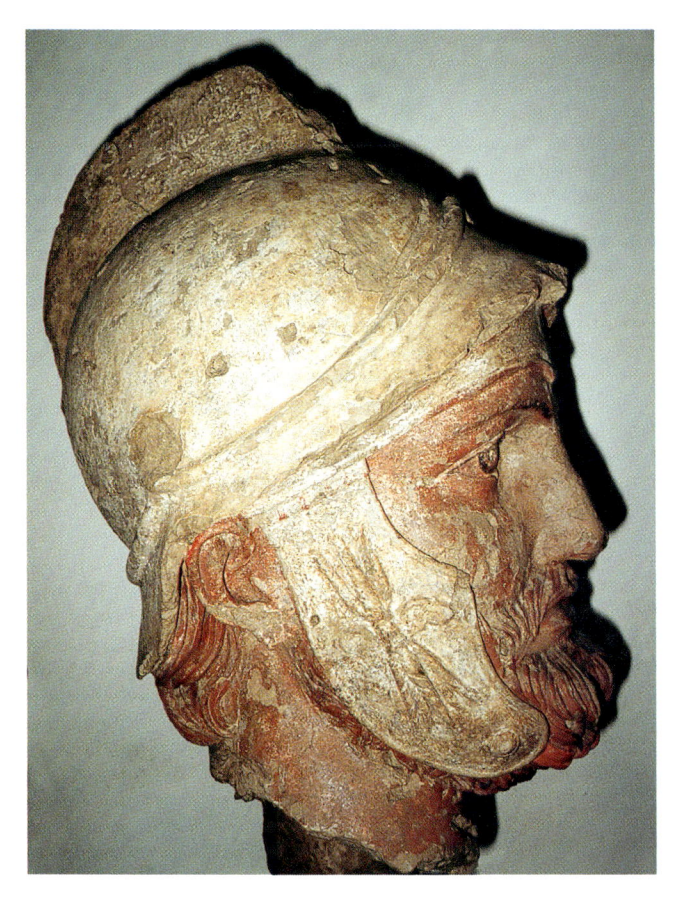

I   Head of a painted statue with helmet, in the Historical Museum, Ashkhabad.

II   Glazed pottery coffin from Warka, in the British Museum.

III   Statue of King Valgash at Hatra.

IV   Relief in the Bel Temple at Palmyra, showing the god Aglibol.

V   Relief at Naqsh-i Rustam showing the investiture of Ardashir.

VI   General view of a Sasanian rock relief (III) at Bishapur.

VII   Relief at Naqsh-i Rustam showing the victory of Shapur over the Romans.

VIII   Relief of Bahram II at Tang-i Qandil.

IX Silver plate, in the British Museum, decorated with a *senmurv*.

X Silver plate, in the British Museum, showing a king hunting stags.

XI Sasanian seal inscribed in Middle Persian 'reliance on god', illustrating a banqueting scene.

XII Late Sasanian stamped pottery jar.

XIII Sasanian cut-glass tube from Nineveh, early seventh century AD.

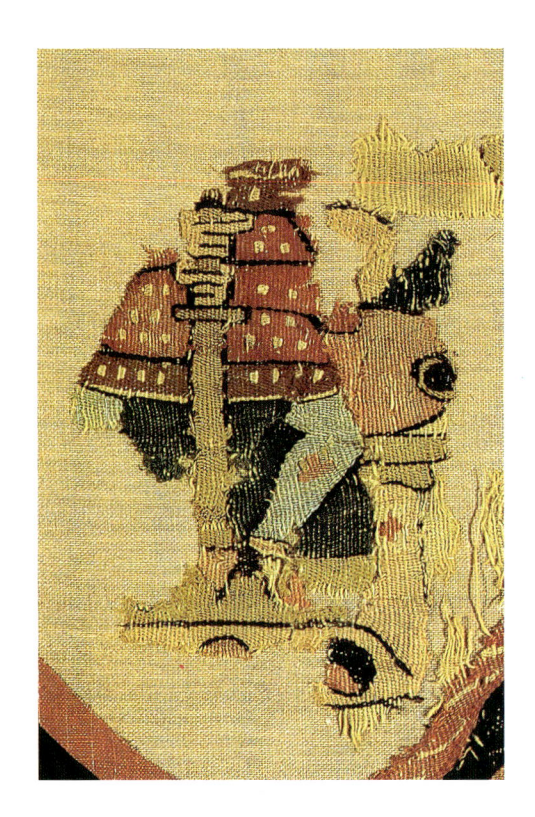

XIV   Detail of woollen textile from Antinoe, Egypt, restored by Mme Dal Pra.

XV   Painted tomb figurines, showing a Central Asian leading a camel loaded with twists of prepared silk fibres. From a Tang tomb in the Xsian region.

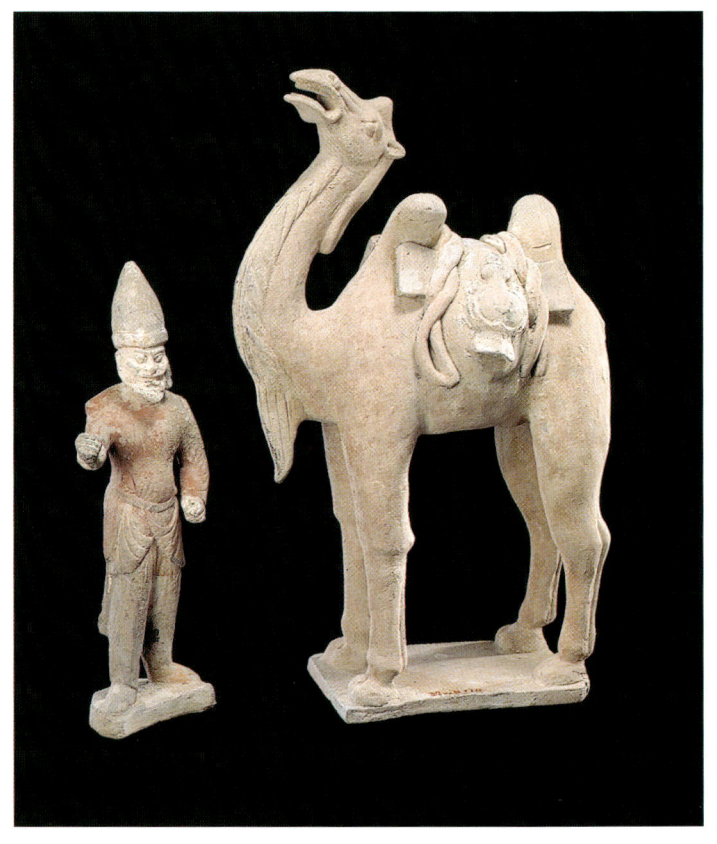

XVI Pottery vessel (height 32.5 cm) with three-colour lead glaze. From a Tang tomb in the region of Xsian.

XVII Addorsed rooster's heads on a Sasanian silk fragment from Antinoe, Egypt.

XVIII A ram on a late Sasanian silk fragment from Antinoe, Egypt.

XIX A winged horse, on a late Sasanian silk fragment from Antinoe, Egypt.